A Storyteller's Guide
to a
GRACE-FILLED
Life
Volume II

Here's what people are saying about Tony:

Tony Agnesi never forgets Who's in charge. The grace of which he writes isn't his to dispense; it comes from God. Agnesi doesn't talk down to his readers; he assumes he's dealing with adults who sincerely seek God, even in the middle of struggles that seem overwhelming. He knows he's not writing for angels.

His tone is a gift to his readers: calm and kind, with just enough edge and challenge to inspire even a temporarily bewildered believer. He's a guide walking alongside the reader, not goading from behind. — **Ellen Kolb, Writer and Pro-Life Blogger**

Books like this speak to many, without alienating anyone. It's just honest, and makes you feel good, without ever demanding you feel a certain way, or his way, about the story at hand.

He skillfully uses his words to start a conversation, and not end one. And man, do we need more of that in our world today. —**Scott Wynn, WQMX Radio.**

The real reason Tony's book rings with authenticity is that he writes about what he knows, what he has experienced as a child, husband and father, and through his prison and homeless ministry.

Every time Tony offers advice, the reader knows experience and his own personal struggles to grow in the Lord are the foundation for his wisdom. —**Melanie Jean Juneau, Editor, Catholic Stand**

Tony relates time and again our innate need to feel loved, and be reminded of our self-worth, despite the circumstances we might find ourselves in. Grace calls our name, and provides the reassurance that God loves us regardless of the past and ushers in the hope of change. —**Elizabeth Reardon, Theologyisaverb.com**

Anyone wanting to grow in virtue will enjoy reading this book! Be assured, Tony Agnesi will make you laugh, cry and close the book wanting more! His writing will touch your heart. — **Virginia Lieto, Author and Blogger at VirginiaLieto.com**

Rare is the successful storyteller who draws an audience by simply sharing his every day journey to make sense of his own life while conscious of the needs and struggles of the people he encounters on the street, at Church, in a pharmacy, at a restaurant, in jail, or while battling cancer.**—Michael Seagriff, Author and Blogger at Harvesting the Fruits of Contemplation**

A Storyteller's Guide
to a
GRACE-FILLED
Life
Volume II

Tony Agnesi

Virtu Press

Wadsworth, Ohio

Printed in the United States of America

ISBN-13: 978-0-578-54937-8 (Virtu Press)

The author is donating 100 percent of the net proceeds from this book to the charities and ministries he and his wife support. Many of these charities and ministries are mentioned in his books.

Dedication

To my parents: Tony and Lucy Agnesi. Your faithfulness to God, and each other, were an inspiration to me. I always wanted the happiness and joy you had. I found it with an unwavering faith in Jesus Christ, and his Church, and my wife Diane, with whom I share the same faith and love.

Mauri & Michele!.

All the Best!.

Tony

CONTENTS

Chapter 2- Faith, Family, Friends

Introduction

While I never intended to write an additional volume of stories in the Storyteller's Guide series, I was surprised to find an additional 44 stories on a hard drive that I thought I erased. The "lost stories" became the name I gave them, until I decided that a Volume 2 of the original book was the best way to present these stories, reflections and meditations. They complete the writing that I did between 2012 and 2016.

The first chapter in the book is *God's Grace in Daily Life*. If we are open to God's grace, we can find Him in our everyday experiences. All we need to do is to be open to the nudges and bumps of the Holy Spirit and have the courage to act on them.

Much of the graces discussed in Volume 1 were those that come to us through our family and friends, and when we are all together. The holidays are a particularly great time to share and recall fond memories of family members who, both came before us and, are celebrating with us now. We pick up on that theme in the second chapter.

As in each of the other books, most stories have a piece of scripture highlighted, followed by a few questions for reflection. The stories can be read all at once, or individually. Some people use the guides for daily meditation. Many prayer groups will use a story, or two, in each group meeting as a conversation starter. I had the opportunity to sit in on a couple of prayer group meetings where my books were used. The stories shared by the group members have been a blessing to me.

Recalling the stories of your own life and sharing them with others is a beautiful way of showing God's grace in your life to others and inspire them to reflect and recall their own family stories. In that way, we can all be inspired by each other, as we grow in our love of The Lord.

I pray these stories will be a blessing to you on your journey.

Christ's Peace,

Tony Agnesi

CHAPTER ONE

GOD'S GRACE IN DAILY LIFE

Why Are We So Angry?

> For anyone who does not love his
> brother, whom he has seen, cannot
> love God, whom he has not seen. —
> 1 John 4:20 (NAB)

It seems like rage is all the rage these days. We have road rage, airport rage, movie theater rage, and school rage. Almost every day we watch television reports about someone who's lost it!

Instead of the internet bringing us closer together, it gives a free and easy platform for the polarization of opinions to the extremes! We communicate via name calling instead of using reason. We choose up sides. If you don't agree with my side of an issue then you are stupid, narrow minded, or a bigot. Intolerance runs rampant!

A recent poll said that over half of Americans say that anger keeps them from sleeping. Nearly one in five say that anger has ruined their marriages or affected their sex lives. [1]

So, why are we so angry?

One opinion is that we are so self-centered, and our feeling of entitlement is so strong that our expectations are higher than ever. We expect everything to go our way, to be perfect, to make us happy. So, when a waitress brings us the wrong beverage, a flight is cancelled, or a customer takes too long at the supermarket checkout, we go ballistic! We see it as a threat to our dignity, an insult, that we somehow have been demeaned. I have a RIGHT to expect perfection!

In addition to our higher expectations, Americans have the highest stress levels in history. And, stress reduces our tolerance for anything that slows us down, gets in our way, or threatens our self-esteem.

We are always in a hurry, multitasking: Driving while reading e-mail, watching television while playing Candy Crush, and talking on the phone, all at the same time. If one thing goes wrong, and it will, we get angry.

We heap this stress on our kids, as well. We have them so involved in school choir, soccer, cheerleading, gymnastics, Spanish club, or any of a hundred other activities, that we jump from one stressful situation to another, adding to their stress, instead of letting them be kids and enjoy a stress free lifestyle by keeping the organized activities to a selected few that they really enjoy.

How do we stop this alarming trend? How do we return to "Love thy Neighbor?" And more importantly, how can we possibly love a God we don't see when we are angry with our brother that we do see?

Here are just a few ideas:

1. **Slow down.** Life doesn't have to happen at 100 mph. Enjoy the peace that comes from silence. Take a walk, read a book, pray, or just sit in silence for a few minutes.

2. **Put the smart phone down!** I am surprised at the number of people who have their smart phone in their hands 24 hours a day. They even sleep with it by their pillow, not to miss a text message, or e-mail. Stop it! I leave my phone charging on the kitchen counter as soon as I get home from work. No smart phone at night, for me, and never in the bedroom!

3. **Check e-mail only two or three times a day.** The reply can wait. We don't need to respond to every e-mail, or text message, right now! And when you do check it, process your inbox to empty. Then, stick to the plan.

4. **Limit your kid's activities** to the top few things they really enjoy. Having fun playing a sport is destroyed when they have three more activities they've got to get to today.

5. **Show some kindness and consideration.** Lower your expectations about perfection. That waitress who got your order wrong is stressed, too. Give her a break, treat her with respect, and your service will improve. I have had several waitresses tell me they are afraid to wait on certain customers. They look for customers who treat them with respect and cut them some slack. You'll be amazed at the great service you'll get.

6. **Be Humble.** Don't take your frustrations out on others. Humility doesn't mean you think less of yourself, but that you think of yourself less.

Let's try to replace our anger with kindness and gratitude. Maybe together, we can help make this a more peaceful world, with God's help.

Reflection: Is anger a problem we all face today? Why do you think people are so angry? Is road rage and movie theater rage a symptom of a bigger problem? Can you offer some solutions?

Close Personal Relationship

> So humble yourselves under the mighty hand of God, that he may exalt you in due time. Cast all your worries upon him because he cares for you. — 1 Peter 5:6-7 (NAB)

Occasionally, an Evangelical friend, or acquaintance, will ask the question, "Do you have a close personal relationship with Jesus?" This question throws many Catholics into a dazed look with no idea of how to answer. The Evangelical friend will gaze back with that "I've got something you Catholics don't look," and the conversation ends there.

It's a good question! For my Catholic friends, here is a way we can examine the question in our own lives and be able to answer their question honestly. Do I have a close personal relationship with Jesus?

First it is important to understand what Evangelicals mean by a personal relationship. They view Catholics as impersonal because of the rituals and hierarchy. A personal relationship to them is the ability to interpret the Bible for themselves and to determine what is and isn't the truth. It's just me and Jesus they will say.

Logic tells us that if everyone can determine their own truth, then it's not the truth! There can only be one truth, and it is found in the Catholic Church.

> There is a God shaped vacuum in the heart of every man which cannot be filled by any created thing, but only by God, the Creator, made known through Jesus. — Blaise Pascal [2]

Here are four ways for Catholics to have a close relationship with our Lord,

1. **Prayer.** When we have a relationship with a friend, we want to speak with that friend often. We call them, text them, get together, whenever we can. Prayer is our connection to Jesus. It is our on-going conversation with a friend.

2. **The Sacraments.** What can be more personal that receiving Jesus in the Eucharist at Mass? Each time I receive the Eucharist at Holy Communion, I have Jesus in me. You can't get much closer than that! The same holds true for the sacrament of Reconciliation where we share our sins and failings and receive forgiveness. Isn't that what happens in a close relationship?

3. **In Scripture.** As we read the Bible, especially the Gospels, we get a closer understanding of the life of Jesus, and the magnitude of what he did for you and me personally by his life, death, and resurrection.

4. **In adoration.** There is not a more beautiful way to have a relationship with Jesus than to adore him regularly in front of the Blessed Sacrament. Visiting our Savior, spending an hour is conversation with Him, and doing it frequently, now that's a close personal relationship!

So, how did you measure up?

Need some help with your **prayer** life? Then, start small. Try praying the morning offering, read today's Gospel, or pray the Chaplet of Divine Mercy on your way to work (best 10 minutes you'll ever spend driving to work). Then, try to add and build upon that start. The more you talk to Jesus, in prayer, the closer your relationship will be.

How often are you receiving the **Sacraments**? Are you going to Mass each week? Have you ever considered a second Mass during the week? Many churches have a noon Mass you can attend, and still have enough time to stop for lunch. Are you going to confession once a year (at a minimum)? Why not make it twice, or even monthly?

Do you find reading **Scripture** a daunting task? Then, why not start with the daily mass readings, or a good Bible app on your smart phone?

Have you ever spent an hour in **Adoration** before the Blessed Sacrament? Many churches offer it on a routine basis. Some, like my parish, offer perpetual adoration, 24/7, and invite adorers to stop in at any time. My wife, who has made a weekly holy hour for nearly 20 years, will tell you it's her favorite hour of the week. A weekly hour with Jesus - that's a close personal relationship.

Now, you have an answer to the question. I pray that you will constantly work to develop a close relationship with Jesus. And, please pray that I will, too, so we both might have a better relationship with our Lord.

So, the next time we are asked, "Do you have a close personal relationship with Jesus?" We can answer, "You bet I do!"

Reflection: What about you? -Do you have a close personal relationship with Jesus? How do you define a close personal relationship? What about Tony's suggestions? Have you tried any of them?

The Devil on My Shoulder

An Old Cherokee told his grandson, "My son, there is a battle between two wolves inside us all. One is Evil. It is anger, jealousy, greed, resentment, inferiority, lies and ego. The other is Good. It is joy, peace, love, hope, humility kindness, empathy and truth." The boy thought about it and asked, "Grandfather, which wolf wins?" The old man quietly replied, "The one you feed." [3]

I remembered as a kid the cartoon that depicted the devil on one shoulder and an angel on the other. The devil whispers in one ear and the angel in the other. The devil suggests sin and the angel suggests goodness.

The devil represented temptation, and the angel our moral conscience.

Do you sometimes feel like you hear two conflicting voices?

I know that I do. We feel torn between what is righteous and what is expedient and feels good. And, often the devil wins! Even though we know what we are doing is wrong, or could have consequences, we do it anyway.

That is the definition of sin! Every time we listen to the devil, instead of the angel, we commit sin. Some sins are small, venial sins but others are more serious, grave sins.

> Consequently, brothers, we are not debtors to the flesh, to live according to the flesh. For if you live according to the flesh, you will die, but if by the spirit you put to death the deeds of the body, you will live.
> Romans 8:12-13 (NAB)

Often, we feel bad about our choices, after the fact. We realize that we were weak, lacking the strength to choose what is morally correct.

Let's face it, we are all sinners. We all make bad choices, from time to time, and we all fall short of perfection. We have a sin batting average, and if we are honest, it could be better.

That's why I like the old Cherokee saying. The grandfather understands that there is a constant fight in each of us between good and evil. And the one that wins is the one we feed. How do we feed this good wolf, make better choices, sin less, and improve our batting average?

Here are a few things that will help:

1. **Pray.** When tempted, pause and pray. It could be a simple prayer as in "God help me," which might be just enough to help us make a clear decision.

2. **Read Scripture.** We find story after story in the bible of people who have made grave mistakes, repented and changed their lives. They went from making bad decisions to making good ones. They improved their averages.

3. **Choose better friends**. As my dad often said, "You become the type of person you hang out with." If we choose friends that avoid sin, it will eventually help us to avoid sin, as well. Sometimes there is one person, one place, one website, one hangout that is the constant cause for our sins. Avoiding that person, place, or circumstance makes it easier for us to stay on the right path. In jail ministry, I often talk to people who have been arrested on drug charges, who decide to live a clean life, only to return to the same friends, same bar or house, with the mistaken ideas that they can say "no." It may take a while, but they will eventually succumb to the peer pressure and do drugs again. The way to stay clean is to find new friends, new hangouts, and a healthy lifestyle.

4. **Frequently receive the Sacraments.** For me, the more often I go to Mass and receive the Eucharist, the better I am a resisting sin. I can't explain why, but it just works!

This week let's make a conscious effort to feed the good wolf, to improve our sin batting average, and to try to live a more righteous, virtuous, and moral life. Let's move away from darkness toward the light, away from the devil and closer to God.

Reflection: *Do you feel this struggle with the wolves within you? Is there one person, place or thing that you need to avoid? What can you do to move toward the light and away from darkness?*

We Celebrate

Hallelujah! Praise God in his holy sanctuary; give praise in the mighty dome of heaven. Give praise for his mighty deeds, praise him for his great majesty. Give praise with blasts upon the horn, praise him with harp and lyre. Give praise with tambourines and dance, praise him with strings and pipes. Give praise with crashing cymbals, praise him with sounding cymbals. Let everything that has breath give praise to the LORD! Hallelujah! Psalm 150 1-6 (NAB)

A few months ago, Diane and I had a very busy weekend. We celebrated the baptism of our niece's son. We celebrated the lives of a husband and wife who died only hours apart. And, we celebrated our mutual birthday (we were both born on February 23rd) with four other couples that share the same birthday week, an annual tradition for over 20 years.

We celebrated three completely different events in just over 24 hours. One was the happy celebration of new life in baptism. One was the very sad celebration of the lives and passing of two cherished friends. And, one was the marking of time with a birthday dinner.

As Christians, especially Catholics, we celebrate many things; births, deaths, marriages, baptisms, the Eucharist, Mass, and the lives of the saints.

All of these celebrations remind me of a book by Matthew Kelly, titled, *Rediscovering Catholicism*. He has a chapter entitled, *We Become What We Celebrate.* [4] It's true.

What we celebrate as a culture is what we become. And, what are we celebrating? We celebrate the bad behavior of Hollywood celebrities, the selfish, self-centered spoiled lives of the housewives of New York. We celebrate lifestyles and attitudes that would be unheard of 50 years ago. We call this progress.

Do you ever wonder what atheists and agnostics celebrate? It seems to me like they steal Christian holidays and make them their own secular ones. Christmas to them becomes trees, twinkle lights and gift exchanges. Easter becomes bunnies and chocolate. Birthdays mark time, and deaths merely mark the final moments before we become worm food. How sad!

> Always be ready to give an explanation to anyone who asks you for a reason for your hope. 1 Peter 3:15 (NAB)

Where is their reason for hope? What is at the center of their celebrations?

For Christians, forgiveness, redemption and salvation give us a reason for hope. Christmas is the birth of our Savior. Easter celebrates Jesus conquering death for our sins. Baptism is the Christian celebration of initiation into God's family and marriage bonds a committed couple in love.

Why, then is Christianity under fire? Why are their fewer and fewer people in the pews on Sunday? Have we failed to make our faith attractive to the people bombarded with anti-life messages? How do we get our message of love across?

As Matthew Kelly writes, the best way to defend life is to celebrate life, and the best way to defend the faith is to celebrate the faith. [5]

We must live our lives to the fullest, never wasting time with things that don't bring us closer to God and one another. We need to live the faith more fully every day, becoming the best versions of ourselves that we can be.

Remember, we become what we celebrate!

Reflection: What do you celebrate? Is a Catholic way of living at the center of every celebration? How do family traditions become your celebration?

Doing vs. Being

> But seek first the kingdom (of God) and his righteousness, and all these things will be given you besides. Do not worry about tomorrow; tomorrow will take care of itself. Sufficient for a day is its own evil. —Matthew 6:33-34 (NAB)

I'm a busy guy. I always work hard, accomplishing more, to pack more projects into my day. Like many Americans, I always worshiped at the altar of productivity. My calendar is always full, often booked 2 years in advance. And, my "to do" list regularly spills over to a second page. I'm so busy doing things that I don't have time to do things! Is this you, too?

Doing is easier that being. Doing is quantifiable. We can measure our productivity in a big promotion, a cleaner house, a better report card, or a bigger paycheck. Doing is what we learn to do from the time we are old enough to understand. Study hard, work hard, and be competitive in your play.

But where is the balance in our lives? After all, we are human beings, not human doings! Many people, in the first half of their lives, spend their health looking for wealth, while in the last half, they spend their wealth looking for health.

Being is different from doing. Being is a feeling, impossible to quantify. It's hard to measure it. The only evidence of it is a sense of peace and well-being.

Psychologists will tell us that we need balance in our lives. We need "doing" time, but we also need "being" time. Finding time to slow down for just being is difficult. On the other hand, at the end of the day, if we have accomplished a lot, but are exhausted, tense, and irritable, then we are out of balance.

Saint Paul tells us to "pray without ceasing" (1 Thes. 5:17) But, where do we find the time? The Catechism of the Catholic Church reminds us that we cannot pray "'at all times' if we do not pray at specific times, consciously willing it." [6]

That's the key! We must dedicate specific times to pray. We need to add them to our calendars, just like any other appointment and we need to stick to them. As Mother Teresa said, "If you are too busy to pray, you are too busy!" [7]

Morning Prayer, evening prayer, grace before meals, Mass on Sundays are all a great place to start. Prayer is the life of a new heart. And, all forms of Christian prayer; vocal, meditative, or contemplative, all have one thing in common; composure of the heart. [8]

For me, whenever I am so busy that my prayer life begins to slip, I can feel my well-being slip as well. And, that's when Mother Teresa's words remind me to slow down, reconnect with my Lord and Savior, and compose my heart to being not doing.

Are you doing or being? As Professor Gordon Dahl puts it, "Americans tend to worship their work, to work at their play, and to play at their worship." [9]

I'm going to make a concerted effort to balance my doing time with my being time.

Join me, let's find that balance together.

Reflections: *Are you doing or being? What do you do to be a more being person? Do you agree that "Americans tend to worship their work, to work at their play, and to play at their worship?"*

Thank God for Crying Babies

> Then children were brought to him that he might lay his hands on them and pray. The disciples rebuked them, but Jesus said, "Let the children come to me, and do not prevent them; for the kingdom of heaven belongs to such as these. — Matthew 19:13-14 (NAB)

I've learned to love it whenever I hear babies cry at church. I like it when a toddler asks his mom a question with a voice so loud to be church worthy. And, my heart warms when I hear the cooing, giggling, and silly baby laughter especially during the quiet time following communion. To me, it's like the angels speaking from heaven.

Sometimes, I think that I am in the minority. Most people frown on crying babies at church. They look annoyed, with their expression of righteous indignation.

Why don't they leave? Why did they come to Mass to disturb those people trying to concentrate? Why aren't they in the cry room? I understand what they are saying. I'd prefer quiet, too!

But, I think there is a bigger question here.

Do you know what it takes to bring children to church? I mean diaper bags, car seats, coloring books, crayons, and the never-ending baggies of cheerios. Parenting at church is tedious, tiring and difficult. And, often, the kids are wonderful for a while, but an hour is just too long for them to sit still.

A priest in the Archdiocese of Washington was in the midst of a homily when a child began to cry uncontrollably. He could tell that the congregation was getting annoyed. But right before people started to leave, he said to the parents, "Don't worry about the crying child. All of that crying just means that the Catholic Church has a future."

He continued addressing the congregation, "If you go into a church that doesn't have a crying baby, the church is in trouble. It has no future. So, let's thank God for crying babies."

As I travel across the country for my job, I attend Mass at many different churches; big churches, small ones, and breathtakingly beautiful ones. But, in many of these churches I don't see small children. In some instances, I have been the youngest person in the pews and I'm officially a senior citizen!

Our Lord loves children. In Matthew 19:13-14, when the children were brought to Jesus that he might lay hands on them and pray, the disciples rebuked them, probably with the same annoyed righteous indignation that I see at Mass. But Jesus told his disciples not to prevent the children from coming to Him. He didn't relegate them to the cry room, the vestibule, or outside. He said let them come to Him.

Do you think when Jesus delivered the Sermon on the Mount there was a cry room? I doubt it! As a matter of fact, I am certain that as he spoke, children were crying, and farm animals were mooing and clucking.

Taking a child he placed it in their midst, and putting his arms around it he said to them, "Whoever receives one child such as this in my name, receives me; and whoever receives me, receives not me but the one who sent me." — Mark 9:36-37 (NAB)

The church is a faith community. And, children are a welcomed part of that community as well. I love the Marty Haugen hymn *"All are Welcome in this Place."* It begins:

Let us build a house where love can dwell and all can safely live. A place where saints and **children** tell how hearts learn to forgive. [10]

When young parents bring their children to church, it's a sacrifice. They do it to teach them the importance of worship and praise. Kids need to learn, and we need to let their parents know that their hard work matters. We need to thank them. Thank them for keeping our faith alive and let them know that they are an important part of our faith community.

Yes, I heard babies crying at church today. Our church is alive! Alleluia! Praise God!

Reflections: *Are you willing to hear some crying to know the church has a future? Do you ever thank a parent for bringing their kids to Mass? As a young parent, do you ever feel unwelcomed at Mass?*

Open the Door to Your Heart

> Behold, I stand at the door and
> knock. If anyone hears my voice
> and opens the door, [then] I will
> enter his house and dine with him,
> and he with me. — Revelation 3:20
> (NAB)

One of my fellow jail ministers, George, likes to use the painting "The Light of the World" by William Holman Hunt [11] to make the point of inviting Jesus into our hearts and lives. It's a wonderful way to illustrate that we must ask Jesus into our lives. Our Lord never forces himself on us. He is always waiting for an invitation to open the door to our heart.

When Hunt painted this piece in the 1850's, he invited his fellow artists to find the mistake in the painting, or better yet, to discover its secret. It took a while but finally a young artist said, "There is no mistake in the painting, but you forgot to paint a handle on the door."

That was the secret. It wasn't a mistake! Hunt intentionally painted the door without a handle to make the point of Revelation 3:20. Jesus stands and knocks at the door of our hearts, but there is no handle on his side. We must invite him in.

Have you invited Jesus into your heart? He is waiting, knocking on the door of your heart, ready to give you a new life that will last forever.

If you examine Hunt's painting closely, you will see additional symbolism. Jesus is still wearing the crown of thorns and his face is sad. He's been knocking at your door for a long time. Why haven't you welcomed Him in? Do you suffer from the "obstinately closed mind" that Hunt said keeps us from a new life in Jesus?

Jesus is carrying a lamp to light the pathway. Are you spending your life in darkness? Jesus invites us into his light, the light of the world. Are you willing to let Jesus be the light of your life?

In front of the door weeds have grown. Do you feel that you are living your life in the weeds? Or, that the weeds are so high that you can barely see the light of day? Jesus is there to remove the weeds. All you need to do is ask.

As with the parable of the prodigal son, all that the repentant son needed to do was make the first move, and his father ran out to meet him.

Jesus is waiting at the door of your heart, knocking patiently. For many of us, he has been knocking for a long time. There is no better time than right now to open the door.

Let Jesus, the light of the world, be the light of your life.

Reflection: *Have you made the first move to meet Jesus waiting at the door of your heart? Do you see the symbolism in the painting?*

Friendship Deficiency

This is my commandment: love one another as I love you. No one has greater love than this, to lay down one's life for one's friends. You are my **friends** if you do what I command you. I no longer call you slaves, because a slave does not know what his master is doing. I have called **you friends,** because I have told you everything I have heard from my Father. It was not you who chose me, but I

who chose you and appointed you to
go and bear fruit that will remain, so
that whatever you ask the Father in
my name he may give you. This I
command you: love one another. —
John 15:12-17 (NAB)

One Thursday morning, waiting for the 8 AM Mass to begin, I realized that I was surrounded by eight male friends. Thursday's are special because after Mass we all go to breakfast together. It's a time to share stories and tell jokes, but it's also a time for prayer and concern for others.

For a moment, I flashed back to a trip Diane, the boys, and I had taken to Italy. As we visited Lake Como, Diane and the boys were enjoying the sites while I slipped away on my own and walked to a nearby *funicolare* (cable car). I took a ride to the top of the mountain, to a small village, called Brunate. As I reached the top, I walked down a sidewalk along the side of the mountain. I enjoyed the breathtaking views of Lake Como below.

Minutes later, I noticed a group of men, sitting at table playing cards, drinking wine and eating pizza. They were laughing, joking and having a fun time. I could tell they were life-long friends.

"Buon giorno il mio amico. Vieni, unisciti a noi!" said an elderly grey-haired man. (Good morning, my friend. Come, join us!)

As I approached, one of the men pointed me to a seat, handed me a slice of pizza and a glass of wine. Within a few minutes we were laughing, communicating with each other, via broken English, and broken Italian. We became instant friends.

Is this the norm? Are these scenes repeated thousands of times each day? I'm afraid not. Male friendships have taken a hit over the years.

A 2006 study found that people in the United States, especially men, had fewer friends than they had 20 years ago. [12] In 1985, men claimed to have three close confidants, 20 years later only two. Friendship is difficult for most men. A good number of men today have one good friend, their wife!

One in four people said they have no one to confide in. That's right, no one!

So, what happened, and what can we do about it?

One thing is time famine. We spend so much time on jobs and careers that there is very little time left for friendship. And, what little time we do have is spent with our spouses and children.

Another factor is that we move, often, for new jobs and creating a need to cultivate new friendships.

Ask any guy right out of college, and they will tell you that as their buddies got married, one by one, their close friendships diminished. Yes, they were still friends, in theory, but rarely get to see one another.

Having strong friends cuts your risk of death by 60%, lowers blood pressure, and increases happiness. Research indicates that women live longer (one of many reasons) because they are better than men at friendships. [13]

> There are friends who bring ruin,
> but there are true friends more loyal
> than a brother. — Proverbs 18:24
> (NAB)

What are some of the things we can do to build better friendships? And, not just golf friends or poker buddies, but true friendships where we can share intimate life details, problems, and shortcomings. We're talking about friends that will hold us accountable for our behavior. They will help us in our relationship with God and with our wives and children.

Here are a few things to try to build better friendships:

1. At work, try to get to know fellow workers and their interests. Ask someone that shares your interests if they want to go out to lunch. And, don't be so quick to turn down requests for lunch or a drink. When you get to know coworkers, they just might become friends.

2. At church, join a men's group, prayer group or bible study. Many of the guys in my men's group have become good friends. They are not afraid to hold me accountable and expect me to do the same for them.

3. At home, try reaching out to old friends. Call them, send them an e-mail, or text them. Time goes by so quickly that it surprises me how rarely I get to see my old friends. Check in with them, set a time to get together, watch a ball game, or meet for lunch. Write it down on your calendar.

4. In your spare time, get out of the house! Many men become couch potatoes, watching football, playing video games, surfing the web. How about joining a gym, taking a class on a subject that interests you, or signing up for a men's basketball or softball team?

Jesus and the apostles give us a fantastic example of male friendship on which to model our own friendships. They truly enjoyed one another's others company, held each other accountable for their actions, and supported each other on their life journey.

My wife is my best friend and that's very special to me. But, having male friends to share my questions, problems, and shortcomings with, who will go out of their way to help me and hold me accountable, that's something special, too!

Reflections: Do you work at making new friends? Do you feel "Friendship Deficient?" What about accountability, do you like it when a friend holds you accountable?

The Power of Yes

Mary said, "Behold, I am the handmaid of the Lord. May it be done to me according to your word." Then the angel departed from her. — Luke 1:38 (NAB)

Such was his intention when, behold, the angel of the Lord appeared to him in a dream and said, "Joseph, son of David, do not be afraid to take Mary your wife into your home. For it is through the Holy Spirit that this child has been conceived in her." — Matthew 1:20 (NAB)

"Yes" is a word with tremendous power. It can unlock amazing opportunities, open doors, and lead us to a richer, fuller and more vibrant life.

In a marriage proposal, it can be the beginning of a lifetime of happiness.

In a job offer, it can be the beginning of a new career.

Saying "yes" to an idea can launch a new discovery, invention or cure.

In the gospel of Luke, a young virgin is asked by the angel Gabriel to bear God's son. Mary was troubled at what the angel said, and she pondered his words carefully. She was confused because she was a virgin.

But, in Mary's troubled confusion, fearful as she pondered what was being said, her response was "may it be done to me according to your word."

Mary said "Yes." Salvation history began with that yes!

> Let us look at her, and let us look to her, in order to be more humble, and even more courageous in following the Word of God, to receive the tender embrace of her son Jesus, an embrace that gives us life, hope, and peace. — Pope Francis [14]

Her betrothed, Joseph was a righteous man. In the gospel of Matthew, not wanting to expose Mary to shame, he decided to divorce her quietly. But when an angel appeared to him in a dream and asked that he take Mary as his wife, his response was "yes!" And, he named him Jesus, just as the angel instructed.

Yes is a powerful word, indeed. It can change the course of history.

Both Mary and Joseph were scared, confused, and felt unworthy. They struggled and pondered what was said and were free to say "no." They trusted God and gave themselves over to God's plan for their lives.

During Advent, God invites us to follow him. However, the decision is ours because of our free will. We are free to choose.

We are scared, feel unworthy, and struggle with what it means to truly follow Jesus. We ponder how our lives will be changed if we trust God and give ourselves over to His plan for our lives.

Do we have the faith to respond to God's call with a "Yes?" Are we willing to take a leap of faith that might lead us to a richer, fuller, more vibrant way of life?

With our "Yes" we can nurture the word of God within us. Like Mary and Joseph, we are called to bring forth a Savior to a weary, troubled world.

We live in a weary world. People are scared, confused, struggling and pondering their own life's decisions. The world is waiting for our "Yes."

Your "yes" can help change the course of history.

Mary and Joseph's "Yes" proposes to each of us a new way to live; a way of surrender to the Word made Flesh who dwells among us here and now.

This advent, let us echo Mary and Joseph's "yes!" Your single "Yes!" might just change the world.

Reflections: *Have you said yes to Jesus? How did Mary and Joseph's yes make you examine your own commitment? How do you say yes, every day to Our Lord?*

More or Less

> Do not conform yourselves to this
> age but be transformed by the re-
> newal of your mind, that you may
> discern what is the will of God, what
> is good and pleasing and perfect. —
> Romans 12:2 (NAB)

I'm not a fan of New Year's resolutions, but I do like to take some time at the end of the year to set goals. Resolutions are great, but we rarely follow through on them and that can make us feel like failures.

Why not try something different this year? Decide what you want to do less, then, find something opposite and positive that you want to do more. Then, take some baby steps in the new direction. Here are a few examples of what I am going to try to do less of this year and what I want to do more.

I want to **complain less and express appreciation more**. There is something addictive about complaining. There is always something to complain about and for many people complaining is what they do all day. What we need to do is focus our attention on appreciation. You might find that there are just as many things to be grateful for as there are things to complain about.

I want to gossip less and praise more. You can always find a group of people who will spend their time gossiping about anyone who isn't there. They suck you in to their conversations, kill your positive attitude and compel you to join in. Learn to counter their gossip with praise. Praise someone who did something nice for you; someone who helped you with a project at work or offered a helping hand when you were in need.

I want to procrastinate less and take action more. It's amazing how fast time passes. That project you were going to do last January never happened. And, now it's a year later and you still haven't begun. Create fewer objectives and get to work on them now. You'll find that you'll get more done by attempting less.

I want to say less and listen more. Often, we have a lot to say and we want to share our knowledge to add to the conversation. We also need to know when to be quiet and listen. People want to share their story, telling you what's going on in their lives. Give them some time to share. You'll find that they will be more interested in what you have to say if you listen first.

I want to eat less and exercise more. This coming year I want to carve out time to exercise and do it. I never miss a meal (hardly ever), so why should I miss an opportunity to get some physical activity? I want to tip the scales to less eating and more activity. As a result, the scale should show a smaller number this time next year.

I want to get angry less and show kindness more. Anger is a banquet and you are the entrée. Anger eats away at you, destroys your health and well-being, and causes stress. Kindness is relaxing. It improves your health and well-being, and calms stress.

I want to judge less and accept more. We love to judge people. We are annoyed by their flaws and misgivings. We need to learn to accept them, flaws and all, just as God accepts us, just as we are, with all our flaws.

> Only if you thoroughly reform your
> ways and your deeds; if each of you
> deals justly with his neighbor; if you
> no longer oppress the resident alien,
> the orphan, and the widow; if you no
> longer shed innocent blood in this
> place, or follow strange gods to your
> own harm, will I remain with you in
> this place, in the land which I gave

your fathers long ago and forever.
— Jeremiah 7:5-7 (NAB)

There are so many other things that I could add.

Watch television less and read more.

Frown less and smile more.

Fear less and love more. I am sure that you can think of many others to add.

This holiday season let's make sure to take some time to set goals. Use that time to think about what you want to change in your life next year. Meditate on what you want to do less and what you want to do more. Write them down and then get to work on making it happen. It will be a gradual change, as less of a negative thing is replaced with a more positive one.

Come on, you can do it! We'll do it together.

Reflections: *What do you want to do more and less? What are a few of your goals for positive change? What changes do you want to make this year?*

Enter into My Rest

> Forty years I loathed that genera-
> tion; I said: "This people's heart
> goes astray; they do not know my
> ways." Therefore, I swore in my an-
> ger: "They shall never enter my
> rest." — Psalm 95:10-11 (NAB)

Every day, as I read Psalm 95 to begin the divine office, the phrase, "enter into my rest" seems to jump off the page.

What is this rest that God speaks of? What did the Israelites do to fail to enter into it? And, more importantly, what can we do to enter into God's rest?

Ultimately, we are talking about that eternal rest with God in Heaven. It was the Israelites disbelief and loss of faith in God that caused them to murmur against him and desire to go back to their slavery under the Egyptians instead of continuing on to the Promised Land. It was not until the next generation, under the leadership of Joshua, that the Israelites entered into the land of Canaan, into God's rest.

Disbelief (not putting their faith in God's hands) is what caused them to not enter into that rest.

What about us? Is God's rest still available to us? How do we enter into that rest?

> Therefore, let us be on our guard while the promise of entering into his rest remains, that none of you seem to have failed. — Hebrews 4:1 (NAB)

The good news is that the promise remains! We have, and continue to receive, the good news through the Gospels. We just need to **believe it.** We need to accept the offer and trust totally in God's promise.

Easier said than done, right?

The truth is, we either trust ourselves to save ourselves, or we trust God, for our salvation through the life, death and resurrection of his Son, Jesus Christ, on the cross. That's your choice!

For many of us, talking a good game isn't the same as living it. We trust in God, to a point, but when the going gets tough we tend to rely on our belief in ourselves to get us through difficult circumstances. We just can't take that final step of surrender that leads to entering into God's rest. We become like the Israelites who hear the word, but just can't surrender totally.

So, what can we do to enter into God's rest?

1. We must realize we can't do it on our own. We need faith through the grace of God. As Ephesians 2:8-9 reminds us, *"For by grace you have been saved through faith, and this is not from you; it is the gift of God; it is not from works, so no one may boast."* We need to accept this gift from God and ask for His grace.

2. We must believe, not just to a point, but total faith in Christ and obedience to his will. Total surrender, putting outcomes in God's hands and not relying on our own devices, is the only way. Anything less and we are no better than our ancestors in the desert.

3. We must encourage each other. As Hebrews 3:13 tells us, *"Encourage yourselves daily while it is still "today," so that none of you may grow hardened by the deceit of sin."* It should be our goal not only to enter into His rest, but also, our spouses, children, family and friends. We need to help each other overcome disbelief. After all, we all have our own moments of disbelief.

4. We must find truth in the Gospels. We must not only receive the Good News but profit from it. As Hebrews 4:2 explains, *"For in fact we have received the good news just as they did. But the word that they heard did not profit them, for they were not united in faith with those who listened."*

5. We must "keep the faith." God's rest is available to all of us. We must be that shining witness to the faith for others. When we "keep the faith" we light the way for others.

We all need God's rest and He offers it to us through His son Jesus Christ. Let's encourage each other to remain faithful in our belief, share the Gospels and together enter into his heavenly rest.

This is my prayer, my friend.

Reflections: *We all need God's rest. How are you entering into His rest? How would you define God's rest? How does faith help us enter into God's rest?*

Overcoming Disappointment

I will never forsake you or abandon
you. — Hebrews 13:5 (NAB)

Let's face it, there is no way around it, we will all experience disappointment. It is a natural and normal part of life. We have high expectations for ourselves and others, but often, we don't live up to those expectations.

Debbie is disappointed that she didn't get the job that she thought was a perfect fit for her skills. She is disappointed in herself, the company and the process. Her disappointment turned into discouragement.

Bill is disappointed that after the undefeated season his baseball team enjoyed, they lost in the finals to a team they should have beaten. Bill is disappointed in himself, his teammates and coaches. He questioned whether he should return next season.

Sue thought she and Tom had the perfect marriage until the day Tom announced he was leaving her and the kids because he had fallen in love with his secretary. Sue's disappointment turned quickly to depression and desperation.

Brian anxiously awaited the results from his surgery. He was disappointed when the surgeon told him that the cancer was worse than they expected. He was disappointed with the doctor and discouraged and angry with God.

Yes, we all experience disappointment.

So, what can we do when we this happens? And, how do we keep from becoming discouraged or depressed?

Here are some thoughts:

1. **Take some time to grieve.** Often these disappointments are devastating. They require time to heal, to reflect, and to comprehend. Know, however, as St. Paul tells us in Romans, *"We know that all things work for good for those who love God, who are called according to his purpose." (8:28)*

2. **Examine our perspective and expectations.** We have high expectations for others. And, often people won't live up to our vision of them. This is especially true for family members. We sometimes have unrealistic expectations for our children, spouses and parents. When you have overly high expectations, you set yourself up for disappointment. Put your expectations into their proper perspective.

3. **Turn toward, and not away from, God.** When people are discouraged, they often make the mistake of blaming God, of going into a shell, no longer attending church and they stop praying. These are the very times that we should turn toward our Lord. By doing so, we gain strength from His promise to us, that He is with us always, that He will never abandon us, that He will see us through the problem and gives us a way out.

4. **Focus on hope.** We need to put our faith in God that he will give us a reason to hope. If we dwell on our Lord, and not on the disappointment, we will begin to see that there is a light at the end of the tunnel. And, that light begins with our hope.

   > Rejoice in hope, endure in affliction, persevere in prayer. — Romans 12:12 (NAB)

5. **Be grateful for the good things in your life.** Often, we spend so much time on our problems and disappointments that we fail to take stock of our blessings. We may have lost

out on that job, but there will be other opportunities and we still have our God given skills. We may be disappointed at losing the big game, but we still have a season full of good memories to motivate us next year. *In all circumstances give thanks, for this is the will of God for you in Christ Jesus. --1 Thessalonians 5:18*

We all face disappointments during our lives. Dealing with disappointments, by trusting in God and His promises, will go a long way to improving your mental health and happiness.

You are in my daily prayers, my friend.

Reflections: *So, what can we do when we experience disappointment? Do you have a way of coping with disappointment that works for you? Do you ever find yourself blaming God for your disappointments?*

Old Wineskins

> Likewise, no one pours new wine into old wineskins. Otherwise, the new wine will burst the skins, and it will be spilled, and the skins will be ruined. Rather, new wine must be poured into fresh wineskins. [And] no one who has been drinking old wine desires new, for he says, 'The old is good.'" — Luke 5:37-39 (NAB)

There is a saying I have used in business for over 40 years, "You can only coast in one direction." So often, as I talk with new clients they would say, "if only we could keep the status quo, things would be great." The problem with keeping everything the same is that things always change.

People dislike change. The only people that like change are wet babies! It's true.

Nowhere is this resistance to change more prevalent that among some Christians. They want to keep things just the way they were when they were young. The same holds true for Catholics who want to return to Latin, turn the altar away from the people, and return to pre-Vatican II practices.

Sorry to say, you can't put the genie back into the bottle and you can't un-ring a bell. Additionally, the digital world moves too quickly, and business that were once necessary are no longer relevant.

Did you ever think that people would be getting their daily news from Facebook and Twitter instead of the newspaper? Remember record stores or travel agencies? They have been replaced by digital downloads and on-line reservations.

As Jesus taught, you can't put old wine into new wineskins. Jesus had a new way that was different from the ways of the Pharisees and Scribes. Jesus is not suggesting that we change the church teachings, and neither am I. Rather, we must take a hard look at why church attendance is on the decline and why millennials are leaving Christianity in record numbers. We aren't going to get them back by putting old wine in new wineskins. We must find ways to share the apostolic proclamation of salvation through Jesus Christ in ways that reaches a new generation. What got us here won't get us there!

Pope Francis' latest writings point us in this direction. He has a unique understanding of what needs to be done to reach more people with the message of God's mercy. But, unfortunately, good Catholics continue to reject the message, choosing as the Pharisees and scribes did, to cling to their old ways.

That is not to say the old ways are wrong, or bad! In verse 39, Paul tells us that old wine tastes good and that those of us who have tasted the old wine have no desire for the new because the old is good. I can still remember the Latin Mass responses from years as an altar boy, but most priests, ordained since Vatican II, have never said a Mass in Latin. And, while I am old enough to remember, I have no desire to return to Mass in Latin.

Should the Latin Mass be available for those that want it? Absolutely! But, don't mistake it as a tool for evangelization.

So, what can we do to help Pope Francis in his attempt to reach those who have left the faith and invite them to rediscover Jesus and welcome them into our beautiful Catholic faith? Here are a few thoughts:

1. **Is my faith in a rut?** Ask yourself the question, "Have I become tepid in my faith? Am I simply settling for routine?" We just celebrated Lent and Easter. Did you notice? Did you use Lent to shed some of your old self and become a new self in Jesus? Or, was Easter Sunday just another Mass and just another Sunday?

2. **Are you clinging to routine, or resisting change?** In business, when someone says, "That's the way we have always done it," it almost always reflects a resistance to change.

3. **Are you putting Jesus into your old wineskins?** Catholic spirituality is broad, not narrow. Attend Mass in different parts of the country, or different countries, and you will see a faith that has many expressions; some cultural, some ethnic, but all with the same message of Jesus' life death and resurrection; of salvation through our relationship with Jesus.

Jesus asks us to open our hearts anew, to be shining examples of Jesus' love, to invite family and friends to rediscover the Catholic faith and share our joy with the world.

Let's enjoy the vintage wine, aged to perfection, but let's not let our satisfaction with the old prevent us from sampling the new. And, let's not be critical of those who evangelize with the wineskins of new hearts, new lives, and salvation through our savior, Jesus Christ.

Reflections: *Are you guilty of clinging to the old and familiar? How can we reflect on younger Catholics and find ways to communicate with them in a way* *that makes our faith attractive? Are you guilty of the saying, "if we could only keep things the way they were?"*

Are You the One?

> When John heard in prison of the works of the Messiah, he sent his disciples to him with this question, "Are you the one who is to come, or should we look for another?" — Matthew 11:2-3 (NAB)

Doubts We all have them at times. As Christians, we are embarrassed by our doubt. Is the story of Jesus true? Did he really die for my sins?

Noah had doubts when he built the Ark.

Abraham had doubts when he offered to sacrifice his son Isaac.

Moses had doubts when he led his people across the Red Sea.

David had doubts when he faced Goliath.

We know Blessed Mother Teresa had doubts, as she wrote about her "dark night of the soul."

Even John the Baptist, arguably the greatest prophet of the bible asked the Lord, "are you the one who is to come?"

Jesus, in Matthew's gospel, said that "among those born of women there has been none greater than John the Baptist." (Matthew 11:11) Yet, as John rotted away in prison, even he had doubts.

As we prepare for the coming of Jesus during Advent, we can use this time to read, study, talk to friends who have a strong faith, confess our sins and recommit ourselves to living a Christ-like life.

> "Everything is possible to one who has faith." Then the boy's father cried out, "I do believe, help my unbelief!" — Mark 9:23-24 (NAB)

What most people fail to realize is that doubt is not the opposite of faith. Disbelief is the opposite of faith. Doubt can actually build our faith and be the catalyst for spiritual growth, because it causes us to question things, and as a result learn truth.

Doubt is not sinful and unforgivable. God is big enough to handle all our questions. Doubt does not indicate a lack of faith, but a desire to have our faith grow.

Here are a few things to remember:

God is kind and merciful. He is patient with us and wants us more than we know. Like the father of the prodigal son, all we need to do is move in his direction and He will rush to greet us!

> So, he got up and went back to his father. While he was still a long way off, his father caught sight of him, and was filled with compassion. He ran to his son, embraced him and kissed him. — Luke 15:20 (NAB)

Our struggles bring new growth in faith. If we are doubt-free, we must already be in heaven! As for us earthlings, if we move in the direction of light, and not darkness, then, even in our doubt, we move closer to God.

In prayer, it's OK to admit our doubt and tell God how we feel. We can ask God to "help my disbelief." God will never give up on us. In His compassion and patience, He will wait for us and bless our searching.

Advent is a time to discover a closer and more intimate relationship with our Lord; to confront our doubts and turn them into a stronger, more vibrant faith. By doing so, we can then answer John the Baptist's question, "Are you the one?" with a resounding "Yes!"

On Christmas morning, Jesus, the One, has come into the world, our Savior, born of a virgin in Bethlehem.

Halleluiah!

Reflections: *Do you think your doubt is a lack of faith? What do you think of Tony's idea that doubt can lead to a greater faith? What will you be doing during Advent to grow your faith?*

Rush to Judgment

It's easy to look at people and make quick judgments about them, their present and their past, but you would be amazed at the pain and tears a single smile hides. What a person shows to the world is only one tiny facet of the iceberg hidden from sight. And more often than not it's lined with cracks and scars that go all the way to the foundation of their soul. Never judge, learn to respect and acknowledge the feelings of others. — Sherrilyn Kenyon[15]

The news headlines are full of accusations, judgments, and jumped-to-conclusion statements. Innocent until proven guilty has been replaced by the court of popular opinion.

It seems that the more famous the person, the quicker we rush to judge him. We love to build people up, only to cut them down as soon as something bad happens.

We place professional athletes on a pedestal. We hero worship them, at least until they throw an interception, miss a free throw or strike out. Then, we look for any reason to pass judgment. We have no facts, just our bias and uniformed opinion.

We do the same thing with family members, friends, coworkers, and neighbors. We quickly pick up the latest rumor, juicy information and harmful gossip.

> You know my name but not my story. You've heard what I've done not what I have been through. Go ahead judge me, but you will never understand me until you've walked a mile in my shoes, and I wouldn't wish that on anyone. —Jonathan Anthony Burkett [16]

The problem is we don't know another's story. We have no idea what they are going through, what challenges and hardships they face, what pain they feel. As the old saying goes, we haven't walked a mile in their shoes.

The man, who cut you off on your way to work this morning, just received the news that he has cancer.

The woman at the checkout counter, who was curt and sassy to the cashier, just found out that her husband is having an affair.

The kid that failed the math test just had her world turned upside down discovering that her parents were getting a divorce.

How would we react in the same situations? Would we want, or even expect, the benefit of the doubt? If they only knew what I was going through!

Instead of the modern-day court of public opinion, fueled by the secular media, what is the proper Christian response to situations that we are bombarded with?

> Judge not, that you be not judged. For with the judgment you pronounce you will be judged, and with the measure you use it will be measured to you. (Matt 7:1-2 NAB)

> Stop judging and you will not be judged. Stop condemning and you will not be condemned. Forgive and you will be forgiven. (Luke 6:37 NAB)

Example after example in James, Romans and Ephesians drive home this point. We are not to judge, condemning, gossiping, and spreading nasty rumors.

> We can never judge the lives of others, because each person knows only their own pain and renunciation. It's one thing to feel that you are on the right path, but it's another to think that yours is the only path. — Paulo Coelho [17]

We are to "walk a mile" in their shoes, get to know the real story, the whole story, the pain behind their behavior, and maybe then, we will have a greater understanding of their situation.

We never know the battle that people are fighting. As author Sherrilyn Kenyon reminds us, we would be amazed at the amount of pain and tears a single smile hides. Let's try not to be one of those people who quickly to rushes to judgment.

Reflections: *Are you quick to judge? Do you find that you gossip? Do you ever consider walking a mile in someone else's shoes?*

What Defines Character?

> You are the salt of the earth. But if salt loses its taste, with what can it be seasoned? It is no longer good for anything but to be thrown out and trampled underfoot. You are the light of the world. A city set on a mountain cannot be hidden. Nor do they light a lamp and then put it under a bushel basket; it is set on a lampstand, where it gives light to all in the house. Just so, your light must shine before others, that they may see your good deeds and glorify your heavenly Father. —Matthew 5:13-16 (NAB)

The dictionary defines character as the mental and moral qualities distinctive to an individual. It's our defining presence, honed by our actions, integrity, honesty, and the choices we make. Our character is one of the few things in life that can't be taken away from us.

Then, why is it that we make all sorts of excuses for a person's lack of character. We make excuses for family, friends, coworkers, even clergy. We say, "That's just how he is." Or, "She just can't help herself, it's in her nature."

In jail ministry, I often say that I have never met a bad inmate, just good people who made bad choices; bad choices that define poor character. I tell them they need to work on their choices. Better choices will improve their character.

By the choices we make, we can always strengthen. Just like exercise builds a stronger body, right decisions, built on a set of moral principles, can build our character, and build a stronger soul.

As Christians, we are called to have a Christ-like character. We are called to be the salt of the earth, the light of the world, shining before others.

How can we avoid excuses and build a more Christ-like character?

First, we must **understand what Christian character and integrity are**, and then choose to follow these moral principles. Are we honest? Do we show proper respect for others? Do we make good moral choices, and keep good company?

> Be diligent in these matters, be absorbed in them, so that your progress may be evident to everyone. — 1 Timothy 4:15 (NAB)

Next, we need to **ask ourselves an important question,** "Do I live by these moral principles? Have my past decisions reflected these values? When might I have failed to make the right choices?"

Third, we need to **change our behavior**. We need to control our thoughts. Saint Paul gives some great advice on this topic:

> Finally, brothers, whatever is true, whatever is honorable, whatever is just, whatever is pure, whatever is lovely, whatever is gracious, if there is any excellence and if there is

anything worthy of praise, think
about these things. (Phil. 4:8 NAB)

We need to **guard our hearts** as we are reminded in Proverbs 4:23 *"With all vigilance guard your heart, for in it are the sources of life."*

And finally, we need to **practice making good decisions**. Through practice, we will make better choices. Saint Peter offers us some guiding words:

> For this very reason, make every effort to supplement your faith with virtue, virtue with knowledge, knowledge with self-control, self-control with endurance, endurance with devotion, devotion with mutual affection, mutual affection with love. (2 Peter 1:5-7 NAB)

Character, it's the essence of who we are. If we are going to take the time to work on something, then let it be our character. It's more important that wealth, power or career. As Rick Warren says, *"God is much more concerned about your character than your career, because you will take your character into eternity, but not your career."* [18]

The Bible is full of examples of people who changed their choices and solidified their Christ-like character. Through practice we can too. We can truly be the salt of the earth and light of the world!

Reflections: *What defines character in your opinion? How important is character to you? Do you have friends whose character you would challenge? If so, why?*

Who are You?

> But you are "a chosen race, a royal priesthood, a holy nation, a people of his own, so that you may announce the praises" of him who called you out of darkness into his wonderful light. — 1 Peter 2:9 (NAB)

Have you ever asked yourself the question, "Who am I?" What are the things that most define your personal identity? What are your talents, passions, and strengths? Our identities often determine our actions, how we live our lives, relate to family and friends, conduct business, and worship God.

Some people define who they are by their **circumstances**. I'm unemployed, a divorcee, diabetic, disabled, or from a dysfunctional family. Circumstances can change, and these are just descriptions that can hold us back.

Some people define who they are by **what they do**. I'm a stockbroker, an avid golfer, a stay at home mom, a realtor. Like circumstances, what you do can change. Many stay-at-home moms wake up one day and the kids have left for college. Their purpose changes, and many find it tough to form a new identity based on what they do.

When I ask inmates at the jail who they are, they often respond with **what they did, or what they think others think of them.** I'm a drug addict, an alcoholic, or a loser. I'll respond, "That's what you did, that's not who you are! You can change your behavior and become someone new, someone positive."

Others define themselves by their **roles.** I'm the boss, the defensive line coach, a mailman. That's not who you are, those roles can change, too.

So, if your identity is not determined by your circumstances, what you do, what you did, what others think, or your roles, then what defines your identity?

All these things are external; who you are is not only external, but internal. How do you feel about your inner being? Who are you on the inside? This is an important part of your identity as well.

> For we are his handiwork, created in Christ Jesus for the good works that God has prepared in advance, that we should live in them. — Ephesians 2:10 (NAB)

Here is an exercise to try.

1. Make a list of all the things that define you both externally and internally.

2. Eliminate anything that is negative from your list.

3. Scratch off the list those external things that might change in the future.

4. Look at what is left and ask the question, "What remains on my list that really defines me?"

I've done this exercise many times. As a matter of fact, I do it every year around the Christmas and New Year holidays. It has changed over time, but it has been consistent in the past several years.

And, it's not very complicated, it's quite simple. I'm a **Disciple of Jesus, Husband, Father, Grandfather and Servant Leader.** It's not particularly exciting, game changing, or sexy, but I am very comfortable with who I am!

How about you? Give it a try. Discover who you really are. You might just like the real you a whole lot better than the one you portray.

Reflection: Have you tried Tony's idea on discovering the real you? Do you like that person better than the one you portray? What can you do to live the person you really are?

Persistence in Prayer

Then he told them a parable about the necessity for them to pray always without becoming weary. He said, "There was a judge in a certain town who neither feared God nor respected any human being. And a widow in that town used to come to him and say, 'Render a just decision for me against my adversary.' For a long time the judge was unwilling, but eventually he thought, 'While it is true that I neither fear God nor respect any human being, because this widow keeps bothering me I shall deliver a just decision for her lest she finally come and strike me.'" The Lord said, "Pay attention to what the dishonest judge says. Will not God then secure the rights of his chosen ones who call out to him day and night? Will he be slow to answer them? I tell you, he will see to it that justice is done for them speedily. But

> when the Son of Man comes, will he
> find faith on earth? — Luke 18:1-8
> (NAB)

Do you ever feel like your prayers are never answered? Do you wonder if God hears your prayers? If God knows our needs, then why do we need to pray more than once, or at all, for that matter? Wouldn't He just know and answer them?

The parable of the persistent widow offers us some answers. The judge in the parable was a man who didn't fear God or respect anyone. He was in it for himself, the money and the power. So, when the widow asked for a judgment, there was nothing in it for him. So, he was unwilling to help.

The widow was persistent. She approached him many times until he finally gave in and rendered a just judgment.

If the judge listened, then wouldn't God answer those who persistently pray for his help? How much more merciful is God than man? And, wouldn't he do it quickly?

Unlike the judge, God wants to intervene on our behalf. We are His chosen people, His beloved children. He wants to answer our prayers. What God needs from us is our faith.

> Therefore, my beloved brothers, be
> firm, steadfast, always fully devoted
> to the work of the Lord, knowing
> that in the Lord your labor is not in
> vain. — 1 Corinthians 15:58 (NAB)

What can we do to be more persistent in our prayer life?

First, understand that **God hears us**. He is a God of justice, showing no partiality. He hears our cries, and He knows our hearts. He wants to answer us.

Second, **God honors persistence**. Throughout the bible, we read of persistence. Even Jesus was persistent in prayer. At the garden of Gethsemane, Jesus left his disciples and prayed three times. Shouldn't we follow His example?

> Ask and it will be given to you; seek and you will find; knock and the door will be opened to you. For everyone who asks, receives; and the one who seeks, finds; and to the one who knocks, the door will be opened. — Matthew 7:7-8 (NAB)

Third, if we have faith, **God will handle our request**. We must believe that we will get an answer to our prayer. It may not be the answer we want or were expecting, but God will answer our prayers.

The parable concludes with a tough question for each of us; "When Jesus returns will he find faith?" (Luke 18:8)

Do we really believe in answered prayers? Are we willing to persist, to ask, seek and knock?

Dear Lord, I'll keep praying in faith, assured that you will answer me.

Reflections: Do you feel your prayers go unanswered? Does God really hear your prayers? What can you do to be more persistent in your prayer life?

Called to Evangelize

> Always be ready to give an explanation to anyone who asks you for a reason for your hope, but do it with gentleness and reverence, keeping your conscience clear, so that, when

> you are maligned, those who defame your good conduct in Christ may themselves be put to shame. — 1 Peter 3:15-16 (NAB)

As Christians, we are called to witness to Christ's message of love. We are called to share our faith with the people around us. The joy of forgiveness, redemption and salvation through Jesus Christ should be an easy task. After all, we are thankful for our faith and our own forgiveness, redemption and salvation.

So why is evangelization so hard for most Christians? Why are we so afraid to share our beautiful faith with others?

I'm not talking about door to door evangelism or standing on a street corner with a John 3:16 sign. I'm simply talking about seizing the opportunity to speak to someone about Jesus when the opportunity arises.

Ask people how they came to know Christ, and most will tell you it was a one-on-one experience, not via a TV evangelist, or a great sermon, or a book. No, it was someone sharing their faith.

Often, it's a friend or co-worker, teammate, or acquaintance. Sometimes it begins with a simple inquiry as to why you seem so happy, joyful, so different? It's a perfect time to gently evangelize, but all too often we freeze. We simply remain silent, out of fear, and miss the opportunity.

We are fearful that we don't know what to say, or that what we have to say won't be accepted. It might be taken incorrectly. It might be rejected, or it might not be politically correct. And so, we remain silent.

As Christians in a secular society, we are always fearful to speak out. We no longer say, "Merry Christmas." It's been replaced with "Happy Holidays." When someone sneezes, we no long say "God bless you," after all, they might be an atheist and we wouldn't want to offend them or be politically incorrect. We fear rejection, but even Jesus was rejected.

In Matthew 19, a young man approached Jesus and asks what he must do to gain eternal life. When Jesus told him to sell what he had, give it to the poor, and follow him, the young man left saddened because he had many possessions.

If even Jesus was rejected, then why should we be so fearful to share our faith? Earlier in Matthew 5, we learn that our reward will be great in heaven for the rejection we receive on earth.

> For, I am not ashamed of the gospel.
> It is the power of God for the salva-
> tion of everyone who believes. —
> Romans 1:16 (NAB)

Yes, but I don't know what to say. In Luke 12:12, we are given the comfort of knowing that *"the holy Spirit will teach you at that moment what you should say."*

And, it's true! You might not even remember what you said to someone (I rarely do), but through the Holy Spirit you will always have the right words. And, that is a real comfort.

There is a story of a man waiting to enter the gates of heaven when he sees a friend being condemned to hell. As their eyes meet the friend says quietly, "Why didn't you tell me?"

The most effective preachers of the gospel are often ordinary lay people whose lives have been transformed by God's grace. Let's not let fear keep us from opportunities to share the reason for our faith!

Reflections: *Are you reluctant to discuss Jesus for fear of offending someone? Is evangelization something you take seriously? Do you leave evangelization to others more qualified?*

Authentic People

> Do not conform yourselves to this
> age but be transformed by the re-
> newal of your mind, that you may
> discern what is the will of God, what
> is good and pleasing and perfect. —
> Romans 12:2 (NAB)

We all know authentic people. We are attracted to them. They exude kindness and compassion. They don't judge. They are trustworthy, passionate, helpful and genuine.

Yet, in a world where we celebrate narcissistic, self-centered, egotistical behavior, why aren't more people seeking their authentic self? The television schedule is full of programs celebrating the Kardashian's, Real Housewives, and self-centered musical artists who, by default, become today's role models for our youth. We are more concerned with the value of our possessions than the value of our souls.

Authenticity is a word that gets used often in articles, on social media and in conversations. But what is it? And, what defines an authentic person? What makes authentic people different?

Here are ten things that authentic people do differently:

1. **Authentic people express their opinions and feelings**. They never fake their response to "fit in" with the crowd. They don't take it personally if people disagree. Rather, they speak the truth unapologetically. This is particularly true when discussing their faith.

2. **They are driven internally, not externally.** Real authentic people listen to their inner voice. They follow their heart, seek their purpose in life and choose their own career. They

never allow external factors influence their decisions. Prayer and meditation guide their path.

> Since we have gifts that differ according to the grace given to us, let us exercise them: if prophecy, in proportion to the faith; if ministry, in ministering; if one is a teacher, in teaching. — Romans 12:6-7 (NAB)

3. **They have good self-esteem** and appreciate themselves and their accomplishments. They keep their self-esteem at a healthy level, never becoming self-centered and narcissistic. They realize that all they have are gifts from God to use in a positive way. They have unique traits and rituals like daily prayer, Mass attendance, meditation, praying a rosary, all requiring self-discipline.

4. **They choose experiences over things.** Authentic people love to experience life and share those experiences with family and friends. They love sharing those "Kodak moments" with those they love over a bigger house, newer car or the latest iPhone.

5. **They are non-judgmental and always kind**. Authentic people understand that we are all different and come from different traditions and cultures. They celebrate these differences without ever compromising their own deep held beliefs. And, when someone attacks their beliefs, they never take things personally, or react with anger or aggression.

6. **Authentic people make the most of bad situations**. They trust God completely and are free of fear. Understanding that suffering is part of life, they seek to learn from every bad situation, without fear of failure and always trusting in the Lord's plan for their lives.

7. **They support others and always wish them success**. Authentic people love and rejoice in the success of others. They are never jealous when a friend gets a promotion, wins a game, or receives an honor. They wish no one harm.

8. **Authentic people avoid negative people**. They find themselves being attracted to upbeat positive people. When an authentic person is in a crowd of gossipers, they kindly and quickly remove themselves from the situation. Negative people drain energy from a room, and an authentic person intuitively recognizes this quickly and simply leaves.

9. **They seek the soul and not the person**. Authentic people don't care how you dress, what kind of car you drive, or the size of your bank account. They realize that some of the greatest wisdom ever received comes from ordinary people with extraordinary stories and beautiful souls.

> But the LORD said to Samuel: Do not judge from his appearance or from his lofty stature, because I have rejected him. God does not see as a mortal, who sees the appearance. The LORD looks into the heart. — 1 Samuel 16:7 (NAB)

10. **Authentic people hunger for the truth**. They are seekers, always looking for the truth. They read the bible and other great books, attend seminars, workshops, and classes. They realize that life lessons are rarely learned in school. Rather, they are learned in a life-long pursuit of truth and wisdom.

Imagine if we all worked on improving our lives by adopting and developing these common traits. We can, with God's help and a strong desire to be the best most authentic version of ourselves become the people God intended us to be!

Reflections: Who is the most authentic person you know? Do you find that people often try to be someone they aren't? How about you?

It's All About Commitment

> He said in reply, "Have you not read that from the beginning the Creator 'made them male and female' and said, 'For this reason a man shall leave his father and mother and be joined to his wife, and the two shall become one flesh'? So, they are no longer two, but one flesh. Therefore, what God has joined together, no human being must separate." — Matthew 19:4-6 (NAB)

I am a fan of committed marriages. Whenever I hear of a couple celebrating 50, or 40, or even 25 years together it makes me smile. It amplifies the "two become one flesh" commitment we read about in the bible.

With all the talk about gay marriage in the news, I think we miss the boat on what we should really be talking about; commitment! Long term commitment! The "committed to doing whatever it takes to make this relationship work" commitment!

A few years back, Diane and I attended an out of state wedding. The ceremony was beautiful, and the reception was amazing and the wedding cost more money than either of us could ever imagine.

At the reception, I had the opportunity to talk with the groom, whom I had just met, and offered him my wishes for a long and healthy marriage.

"Well, if it doesn't work out, we can always get divorced" he shot back laughingly! His response shocked me because his apparent lack of commitment was obvious. The marriage lasted less than six months.

It is said that between 40% and 50% of all marriages end in divorce and the number is even higher (60%) for second-time marriages. And, the number one reason people get divorced is, you guessed it, commitment. [19]

A 2012 study at UCLA's Relationship Institute, [20] followed 172 couples for 11 years and found that people's understanding of commitment can mean two things.

For some it is *"I really like this relationship and I want it to continue."* And, things go well until there are problems, conflicts, and pressures of life circumstances. Once these things happen, and the relationship isn't going well, the marriage is over.

A deeper understanding of commitment goes like this, *"I'm committed to doing what it takes to make this relationship work."* This kind of commitment requires sacrifices, and couples who are willing to make sacrifices in their relationships become better problem solvers.

Having a great marriage takes work. When the groom at the wedding said, "if IT doesn't work," he missed the point. IT doesn't work, YOU DO!

Here are a few things you can do to have this deeper understanding of commitment.

1. **Pray together.** Ask God for unity in your marriage and ask for the strength to handle life's challenges together.

2. **Tell each other, I love you.** Do it every day, several times a day. Reinforce that you are willing to make those sacrifices necessary to make the marriage work.

3. **Be friends.** Couples who spend time together, genuinely enjoy each other's company. Those who consider their spouse their best friend are willing to go the extra mile when times are tough.

4. **Build family traditions.** Recalling special moments together with family, and each other, are a precious reminder of the love and memories that bind a couple together.

5. **Attend Mass or religious activities together.** Divorce rates are much lower for couples that share their faith experiences together, attend services together, and make their faith a central part of their relationship. As Christians, we call it a Christ Centered Relationship.

6. **Laugh.** You will enjoy each other more when you can find the humor in life during the not so funny situations.

When elderly people are asked, "what was the secret to their long and successful marriage?" They will tell you, "it's commitment!"

Reflections: *Do I have a "do what it takes to make this relationship work" commitment with my spouse? What are the things I do to strengthen my marriage? Do I feel that a Christ-Centered relationship gives me a commitment advantage?*

Lord, Help Me to Endure

> Therefore, we are not discouraged; rather, although our outer self is wasting away, our inner self is being renewed day by day. For this momentary light affliction is producing for us an eternal weight of glory beyond all comparison, as we look not to what is seen but to what is unseen; for what is seen is transitory, but what is unseen is eternal. — 2 Corinthians 4-16:18 (NAB)

Do you ever wake up feeling great, that is, until you try to get out of the bed? Every ache and pain seem to rear its ugly head. You have sore knees, ankles that won't bend, and you slump over from the lower back pain. At that moment, you realize that you are getting older.

I feel this way every morning as I rise to go to morning Mass. As I get older, the things I once took for granted as a younger person have started to affect everything. But then, it's off to Mass, breakfast and on to work.

In 2 Corinthians, Paul tell us that this is going to happen; that our outer self is wasting away, but that we shouldn't be discouraged. As our outer-self wastes away, our inner self renews day by day. I feel renewed following Mass; encouraged, feeling renewed in my faith, and ready to endure the temporary physical pain, for the eternal spiritual glory that lies ahead in heaven.

As our bodies weaken, our spiritual life strengthens, preparing us for the "glory beyond comparison!"

For I am already being poured out
like a libation, and the time of my
departure is at hand. I have com-
peted well; I have finished the race;
I have kept the faith. —2 Timothy
4:6-7 (NAB)

We know that our time on earth is temporary, that we all will die.
As youths, we tend to concentrate on those things that are temporary as well. Only as we age, do we begin to make the connection
and start to concentrate on those things that are eternal.

We experience life in the midst of dying, see glory at the end of
suffering, and fix our eyes on the eternal reality.

Getting older is a blessing. What we lose in our physical bodies we
gain in our spiritual understanding. We understand that while we
shed the temporary, we gain the eternal. Isn't God's plan wonderful?

Reflections: *Have you experienced spiritual growth as your physical health
lessens? Do you find yourself thinking about things that are temporary and not
eternal? Do you agree that getting older is a blessing?*

Watch Your Tongue

For every kind of beast and bird, of
reptile and sea creature, can be
tamed and has been tamed by the
human species, but no human being
can tame the tongue. It is a restless
evil, full of deadly poison. With it we
bless the Lord and Father, and with
it we curse human beings who are
made in the likeness of God. From

> the same mouth come blessing and
> cursing. This need not be so, my
> brothers. — James 3:7-10 (NAB)

Have you ever said something that you've regretted? I have. And, I knew the second it rolled off my tongue that I would. We've said awful things, hurtful things, destructive things; comments that will be remembered for a lifetime. And, in many cases, they were said to the people we love the most; the wife, kids, friends, family, have all been the recipients of the deadly poison of our inability to curb our tongues.

As it says in the book of James, we humans have tamed every kind of beast and bird, reptile, and creature, but we can't tame our tongues.

If we could just learn to watch what we say, our words could be a blessing. Have you ever had someone thank you for an encouraging word you might have spoken years earlier? It happened to me just the other night. A young man approached me at a banquet and told me that I had taught one of his classes almost ten years ago.

"That was the most important class I ever took in school! Your encouragement, kindness, and challenging words really spoke to me. Thank you."

Wow! I can't remember the class, or what I said, but to this young man it was meaningful enough that he sought me out at the event.

> If anyone thinks he is religious and
> does not bridle his tongue but de-
> ceives his heart, his religion is vain.
> - James 1:26 (NAB)

So, how do we bridle our tongues and stop saying things we will regret and say more things that will come back to us as a blessing? Here are a few things we can do.

1. **Ask God for His help.** *Set a guard, LORD, before my mouth, a gate-keeper at my lips. Do not let my heart incline to evil or yield to any sin. I will never feast upon the fine food of evildoers. Psalm 141:3-4 (NAB)*

2. **Think before you speak.** We need to listen more and say less. We need to stop and think before we speak in anger. *Those who guard mouth and tongue guard themselves from trouble. Proverbs 21:23 (NAB)*

3. **Ask forgiveness for your hurtful speech.** When we have said something hurtful, we know it quickly. Apologize right away, before the unkind words have had a chance to sink in. And, mean it! Then, ask our Lord for forgiveness and the help needed to watch what you say. *I said, "I will watch my ways, lest I sin with my tongue; I will keep a muzzle on my mouth." Psalm 39:2 (NAB)*

4. **Take responsibility for your words.** You said them, you own them! Be conscious of what you say. Ask this simple question, "What do I have to lose by being kind?"

5. **Practice speaking positive things.** Offer encouragement, comfort, kindness, love, forgiveness, and grace. The more we are conscious of positive speech, the more we can find situations where we can be a blessing.

We have a choice. For me, hurtful things I have said in the past haunt me. I've said enough for a lifetime. As another proverb says, *Death and life are in the power of the tongue; those who choose one shall eat its fruit. Proverbs 18:21 (NAB)*

Humbly, I want to always choose life! How about you?

Reflections: Has there ever been a time when you said something that you later regretted? How did it make you feel? What have you done to bridle your tongue?

Keith

> Again, [amen,] I say to you, if two of you agree on earth about anything for which they are to pray, it shall be granted to them by my heavenly Father. — Matthew 18:19 (NAB)

You meet a lot of interesting people working with the homeless on the streets. One of my favorites was Keith. He was small, very friendly, soft spoken, with a strong Christian faith. He was well versed in the bible and at one time was an elder in his church.

During our conversations, he would often tell me that there were three things he wanted to accomplish; his goals for the near future. Even though he was homeless he still had goals.

One was to find a job, the second to find a place to live and the third was to become a Catholic at Easter.

"Wow! Pretty good goals," I thought. And, he was well on his way to becoming Catholic because he joined the Right of Christian Initiation for Adults (RCIA) at the inner-city parish where we met, and one of the volunteers there agreed to sponsor him.

Often, over the course of that winter, I would see Keith, either at the Friday night dinner for the homeless offered near the church or at daily Mass that he attended quite frequently.

As winter turned to spring, I lost track of Keith, as often happens with homeless friends that we meet along the way.

That spring, a few weeks after we celebrated the resurrection of Jesus at Easter, my wife, Diane, and I were at the movies. As the show ended and we walked out of the theatre, I heard someone call my name.

There was Keith, dressed in a theatre staff burgundy golf shirt, tending to some spilled popcorn from the kiddie film in the next theatre.

Keith greeted me with a warm smile and a hug. I introduced him to my wife, and we chatted for a moment.

> What you get by achieving your goals, is not as important as what you become by achieving your goals. –Henry David Thoreau [21]

"I did it!" Keith exclaimed. "I became a Catholic at Easter!"

That's wonderful," I replied.

"And, that's not all, the day after Easter, I got this job, and yesterday I moved into my new apartment. It's tiny, but it's great!"

"Wow! Keith you achieved the three things we discussed last winter," I observed.

"Sure did, with the help of God," he said humbly.

"Time to set some new goals," I suggested.

As we neared the exit, I repeated my congratulations, "God bless you, Keith."

"And you too, Tony," as he gave me a wave.

Just like in the spring, I've lost track of Keith. I haven't seen him since. I often wonder if he is still employed, and as winter approaches, I wonder if he still has a warm place to live.

He may lose his job, or apartment, but one thing I know he will never lose is his strong faith that God will provide.

Tiny miracles you might think, but you'll never convince Keith, or me of that. They were an answer to prayer, as Keith and I thanked God for his good fortune.

Reflections: How do you go about setting your goals? How do you feel when you accomplished what you set out to do? What role does your faith have in your goal setting?

Minister to the Jesus in Front of You

For I was hungry and you gave me food, I was thirsty and you gave me drink, a stranger and you welcomed me, naked and you clothed me, ill and you cared for me, in prison and you visited me. Then the righteous will answer him and say, 'Lord, when did we see you hungry and feed you, or thirsty and give you drink? When did we see you a stranger and welcome you, or naked and clothe you? When did we see you ill or in prison, and visit you?' And the king will say to them in reply, 'Amen, I say to you, whatever you did for one of these

least brothers of mine, you did for
me.' - Matthew 25:35-40 (NAB)

It is easy to be overwhelmed by all the inequities of the world. Poverty, homelessness, unemployment, divorce, violence, hunger, depression, all seem too much for any of us to possibly make a difference.

It reminds me of the story of the little girl and the starfish. A little girl was walking down the beach, littered with thousands of starfish that washed up in the surf. One by one she would pick them up and throw then back into the water, returning them to their life in the sea.

An adult passerby notices the little girl and asks her why she continues to try to return the starfish to the ocean.

"There are too many starfish," the adult offers. "You can't possibly make a difference."

The young girl picks up another starfish and throws it into the ocean. She looks at the adult and in an excited voice says, "I made a difference for that one!"

When Blessed Mother Teresa looked into the eyes of a person, she pulled out of the gutter, she saw Jesus Christ.

"They are Jesus. Everyone is Jesus in a distressing disguise."[22]

She never worried about the thousands of people in need, she simply ministered to each one she met, one at a time.

"I give myself to one person at a time," she would say. [23]

When we feel overwhelmed, it is good to follow the example of Mother Teresa and simply minister to the Jesus in front of you.

I can't feed the world, but I can volunteer at a soup kitchen.

I can't solve the unemployment problem, but I can help one person find a job.

I can't cure mental illness, but I can comfort a friend suffering from depression.

I can't cure domestic violence, but I can listen to a friend contemplating divorce.

Every morning, as I receive the Eucharist at Mass, I ask the Lord to put someone in my path today, that He can help through me. And, every day, He does! I just need to be aware, available, and attentive; to forget about the tons of things I need to get done that day, and be present to that one person, at least for a little while.

When a young reporter asked Mother Teresa if the need overwhelmed her, she replied, "The answer is very easy, son. I am with one soul at a time. I choose to be fully present to the person I am with. And as I look at each person's face, I see the face of Christ. I never think about yesterday, today or tomorrow, or an hour from now, when I look into a person's eyes. At that moment, it is never 30,000 people. I give myself to one person at a time." [24]

Like the little girl and the starfish, we can't help everyone. But we can make a difference to someone. One at a time, being totally present, listening and serving, we can minister to the Jesus in front of us.

Reflections: *You can't save the entire world, but you can help one person, or situation. What can you do to help just one person?*

Catholics Come in Many Flavors

> Only conduct yourselves in a man-
> ner worthy of the gospel of Christ,
> so that whether I come and see you
> or remain absent, I will hear of you
> that you are standing firm in one
> spirit, with one mind striving to-
> gether for the faith of the gospel. –
> Phil 1:27 (NAB)

I can't tell you how many times I've heard someone say, "You Catholics are all alike!"

"Are you kidding me?" I'll respond. "Just like Baskin-Robbins,
Catholics come in many flavors."

So, to prove my point, here is my humorous attempt at identifying
some of the flavors of Catholics in America today. I've started a list
with ten. See if you agree with my assessment. You might be able to
add even more. Let's go:

1. *The C&E Catholic–* This is the Catholic who goes to church
only twice a year, Christmas and Easter. They figure if you cover
Jesus's birth and resurrection, all the other stuff in the middle is just
filler. And, everyone knows that these are the holidays when you get
nice gifts, or at least, some chocolate bunnies.

2. *The Match 'em, Hatch 'em, and Dispatch 'em Catholic-* The
only time you see these Catholics in church, are ahead of a bride,
behind a casket, or at a baptism. All three usually involve a reception, party or, at the very least, a mercy meal!

3. *The Dine and Dash Catholic-* These Catholics are at Mass
every Sunday, but not for the entire Mass. They usually strategically
place themselves so that they can receive communion, then dash for

the door before the final prayer and closing hymn. They usually will moan some lame excuse about the parking problem, but in reality, they just want to beat the crowd to get a seat at Denny's before the rest of the congregation gets out of the parking lot. Many of them are firmly convinced that the Methodist minister down the road ends his service five minutes before the Catholic Mass, so that his congregation can get first dibs on the seats at Waffle House. By dashing, they can beat both their own congregation and those darn Methodists and avoid the 30-minute wait for Sunday breakfast.

4. ***The Nice at Mass, but Run You Over, Catholic-*** Not as blatant as the Dine and Dash Crowd, they stay for the concluding hymn, but don't dare get in their way in the parking lot. They might be Christians, but they know that the seating is limited at the Perkins Pancake House and have a good idea that the Dine and Dash crowd is already seated and ordering their omelets.

5. ***Sign Language Catholics-*** They aren't really signing the Mass for the deaf, but you might get that impression. They have a gesture for every response. You know the Catholics that do the big arm swing for the "and with your spirit." And, speaking of arms, they really lift "them up to the Lord." And their "orante posture" during the Lord's Prayer is a sight to behold.

6. ***The Sing Poorly, but Loudly, Catholic-*** They are the ones who appear to be auditioning for American Idol, and really think they are the next Whitney Houston, or Michael Bolton. Usually they are the only person in church who doesn't hear their out of key, pitchy, and disruptive wailing!

7. ***The Excessive Sign of Peace Catholic-*** Do you really need to shake hands with the entire congregation? When you leave your section, cross the isle and continue the handshake until after the communion hymn has ended, I think that might be a little too friendly.

8. *The Free Coffee and Doughnut Fellowship Catholics*– These Catholics know the week and times of every free coffee and dough-nuts event, after Mass. They never miss. You don't see them at the Sunday Masses without the free coffee and doughnuts, and occasionally they will come late for Mass on the days when free coffee and doughnuts are served. They are disliked by the Dine and Dash crowd, because they always park their cars, in unauthorized places, blocking in at least a dozen cars until all the doughnuts are gone!

9. *The I Wish the Mass was in Latin Catholic*– These Catholics do not like anything about the church since Vatican II. They think that if the Mass was only in Latin, all of the world's problems would end. The younger ones never attended a Tridentine Mass, but they wish they had.

10. *The More Catholic than the Pope Catholics*– These Catholics know the General Instruction of the Roman Missal (GIRM) by heart. The GIRM notes the rubrics for conducting the Mass. These Catholics know the difference between the 2003, 2007 and the 2010 versions of the GIRM. They are more than willing to point out to the parish priest, or anyone else who will listen, the litany of liturgical abuses at the parish.

And you thought all Catholics were alike! Now you know better.

Reflections: Do you feel that Catholics get pigeon-holed as all being alike? Is there any truth to Tony's humorous thoughts? Do you feel that we can all have our own spirituality?

Who Do You Say That I Am?

> When Jesus went into the region of
> Caesarea Philippi, he asked his disci-
> ples, "Who do people say that the
> Son of Man is?" They replied,
> "Some say John the Baptist, others
> Elijah, still others Jeremiah or one of
> the prophets." He said to them,
> "But who do you say that I am?" Si-
> mon Peter said in reply, "You are the
> Messiah, the Son of the living
> God."— Matthew 16:13-16 (NAB)

In Matthew's gospel, Jesus asks his disciples **two** questions; who do
the people say that I am? And, who do **YOU** say that I am?

What strikes me as the rationale for Jesus' questions is that people
seem more concerned with following the crowd, than following Jesus.

Recently, it seems that the labels of democrat or republican, liberal
or conservative, straight or gay, takes precedence in the formation
of opinions. The connotations of what these labels represent, seem
to override the teachings of our Christian faith. If we are truly Christian, and we have the Bible and the Magisterium as our guides, then
these labels, and what they represent, should have little importance.

> Right is right even if no one is doing
> it, wrong is wrong, even if everyone
> is doing it. — St. Augustine of
> Hippo [25]

But are they?

I am sure that your mother, or Grandmother, told you more than once, "If all your friends were jumping off a cliff, would you jump too?" Usually, this response comes after you have whined, "But, ALL my friends are doing it!"

You see, when it comes to faith and morals, we can't just go along with prevailing public opinion. Wrong is always wrong, even if everyone agrees!

Let's put all the man-made labels behind God. I am a Christian first, before I am a liberal or conservative, Democrat or Republican, and I have a guide, Jesus, who leads me in the right path.

The modern world says many things about Jesus: He was a really good guy, a prophet, a man ahead of his times, another Moses, Mohammed, or Buddha. You've heard them all. They say nothing about Jesus as God, Our Lord, and Savior.

But, who do you say that Jesus is? If he is your savior, your Lord and God, then, don't you think his teachings should trump the lemmings leading us to this culture of death?

Let's make it a point to be Christians FIRST. And let's see what the Bible has to say about issues, so that it can help us form a true Christian conscience. Then, we will understand the question, who do you say that I am?

Reflections: *Who do you say Jesus is? Who do your friends say that Jesus is? Are you a Christian first, before liberal or conservative?*

Personal, Not Private

> Go, therefore, and make disciples of
> all nations, baptizing them in the
> name of the Father, and of the Son,
> and of the Holy Spirit teaching them
> to observe all that I have com-
> manded you. And behold, I am with
> you always, until the end of the age.
> — Matthew 28:19-20 (NAB)

There seems to be a groundswell of opinion among secularists in the United States today that your religious beliefs should be personal. I agree. My beliefs are very personal.

But the secularists take it one step further. They say that my beliefs should also be private. That is impossible for a Christian!

If I am truly living my faith, then I MUST share it with others. Good news is meant to be shared! It would be a selfish act, and un-Christian-like, not to share my faith.

If we are living our faith, then our actions, the way we treat people, the love we show for others, our respect for the elderly, compassion for the poor, are all public statements of witnessing to Christ. You can't hide your faith, if you are living it!

As St. Francis of Assisi said, *"Preach the Gospel at all times, and when necessary use words."* [26] We share our faith simply by the way we live.

In the Gospel of Matthew, Jesus gave us a commission, to go and make disciples of all nations. We can't live that commission if our beliefs remain private. The secularists know this, I wish more Christians did.

My faith is very personal, but it can never be private. And neither can yours.

Reflections: *Do you agree that it is difficult to keep your faith from public view? If you believe strongly, isn't it hard withholding your faith with others? What about "The Great Commission" to make disciples of all nations? What does this call from Christ mean to you?*

CHAPTER TWO

FAITH, FAMILY, FRIENDS

Life Lessons on the Journey

> Finally, brethren, whatever is true,
> whatever is honorable, whatever is
> right, whatever is pure, whatever is
> lovely, whatever is of good repute,
> if there is any excellence and if any-
> thing worthy of praise, dwell on
> these things. – Phil. 4:8 (NAB)

Last week, I received a note from a reader who asked, "What are some life lessons you would share with your new grandson?" I replied that I began writing my stories with that thought in mind. I asked myself, "Is there anything I can share that might help the next generation avoid some of the pitfalls that I've experienced that would help them lead happier lives?"

As you see, many of these life lessons are themes that I write about often. Each of them has been the subject of several stories. Most are chapter headings in my upcoming book.

If one of these is a topic of interest, feel free to type the key word in the search bar on my website to access more information on that topic.

Here are 14 life lessons from along the journey of life:

1. **Live in the moment.** We spend so much of our lives reliving the past, or anxiously awaiting tomorrow, that we fail to live today. Life is short. It passes us by in the wink of an eye. Life is lived in the moment between each breath. We need to live today, enjoy ourselves today, and drink in today's wonder, savor today's moments.

2. **Relationships are everything.** We need to put our relationships ahead of everything else in our lives; before jobs, homes, cars, hobbies, sports, or smart phones. Our relationship with God, our spouse, children, parents, siblings surpass everything else. We need to be there for our children when they need us. And, remember, friendships require time, attention and cultivation. One of the regrets of the dying is they didn't work at their friendships.

3. **Slow down.** We live in a world that has no patience. We are always moving at the speed of light, often cramming our calendars with so many tasks and appointments that we never give enough time to anything.

4. **Less is more**. We always pursue more; a bigger house, a more expensive car, a bigger television screen, electronics, gadgets, shoes, and clothes. Whenever house cleaning, we find things gathering dust! If we eliminated everything from our homes that gathers dust, we would be surprised at how freeing it feels to have less stuff.

5. **Giving is better than receiving**. This runs contrary to everything the media professes. I promise you there is no better feeling than giving to someone who can never repay you and having a positive effect on that person's life.

6. **Practice gratitude.** If we aren't grateful for what we already have, then how can we expect to be grateful for those things

we want? Start the day with thanking our Lord for life, for the day ahead, for family friends and a job. The greater the gratitude, the greater our happiness.

7. **Be compassionate and show empathy.** Concerns for the suffering and misfortune of others, and the ability to understand and share the feelings of others will motivate us to help those less fortunate.

8. **Be forgiving.** Anger and resentment will harm your health, get in the way of your happiness, and cause you to live in the past. It is said that anger and resentment are like drinking poison and expecting the other person to die. It will kill you if you can't find a way to forgive.

9. **Be passionate**. Over the years, I hired many people. Passion is the one thing that stands out above everything else when considering hiring someone. Find something you really enjoy doing, then, be passionate about it!

10. **Be kind**. The smallest act of kindness can change a person's life forever. It costs nothing to be kind, and it sends a powerful message.

11. **Say I'm sorry.** When you've done something that needs an apology, say it! Don't assume the person knows your feelings. Say I'm sorry and mean it.

12. **Fear is an illusion.** Fear will paralyze you. It will cause you to hesitate or stay embroiled in the wrong situations. The fear of taking action is always debilitating. Take small steps, and build confidence.

13. **Failures are life lessons.** If we don't take action because we fear failure, then we don't understand that failures are simply lessons. Failure often puts you one step closer to success. History is filled with people who failed many times before they succeeded.

14. **Pain is a normal part of life.** We all will experience pain in our lives. Physical pain, mental pain, sickness, injury, a job

loss, a bad marriage or a financial setback. Embrace pain as part of life. Our positive attitudes will do wonders to help us get through the pain.

May God richly bless your personal journey, and may it be filled with happiness, wisdom and joy. That is my sincere prayer.

Reflections: What are the life lessons that you would pass along to your grandchildren? How did these lessons become part of your life? Do you want your grandkids not to have to learn "the hard way" as you did?

Is Chivalry Dead?

> So, whatever you wish that others would do to you, do also to them, for this is the Law and the Prophets. – Matt 7:12 (NAB)

A while back, my nephew and I met for dinner, at the local Olive Garden (his choice). It was right in the middle of their busiest time, on the weekend, with an hour's wait for a table. All the benches were taken.

Shortly after we arrived, a couple, sitting nearby, were called and we just happened to be standing next to them. Quickly, we took the two seats, and both reached for our smart phones, Matthew to play games, and me to check email.

As I looked up, a woman with a small baby in her arms was near us and her mother stood next to her holding the hand of a little girl. My childhood upbringing kicked in as I rose to offer her my seat.

With baby in arms, she looked at me and said, "Really? Take your seat?" "Sure," I replied, as she looked at me with disbelief. My nephew, spotting her mom holding the young girl's hand, quickly stood and made room for them to sit.

As the mother took her seat, she said to us, "Thank you, I thought chivalry was dead!"

Growing up in the 50's, we were taught manners. Here are a few things we learned that are missing in today's society:

- We held the door open for other people, especially if they carried a child, or groceries.
- We helped the elderly cross the street.
- We made eye contact with people.
- We said hello to acknowledge people, when they entered the room.
- We offered our seat on the bus to an elderly person.
- We greeted people with a firm handshake.
- We said, "good morning" and "have a nice day."

What has happened? Some young people don't even acknowledge Grandma with the courtesy of making eye contact, or saying hello, never lifting their head from the video game, or smart phone.

Do parents still teach their kids manners? If not, is it because they think their kids are "the center of the Universe" and they no longer need to acknowledge others? Has child raising come to this?

What we need are the good old department store charm schools of the 50's and 60's. Every young girl wanted to go! Also, it was a time when fathers would think less of their sons if they didn't help the older neighbor carry her groceries or open the door when your date got into the passenger seat of the car.

"The Golden Rule" or the "Ethic of Reciprocity" has a basis in al-most every world religion. It can also be explained with Philosophy,

Sociology, or Psychology. The concept predates the term "Golden Rule" which became popular in the1600's.

In the bible, we have a form of this in a couple of passages:

> Take no revenge and cherish no grudge against your fellow country-men. You shall love your neighbor as yourself. I am the LORD. - Le-viticus 19:18 (NAB)

> Do to others as you would have them do to you. - Luke 6:31 (NAB)

So, what went wrong? Are we so into ourselves that we can't acknowledge others, offer them a greeting, look them in the eye, assist them when they need help? If we were treating our neighbors as ourselves, then these questions would be moot.

Let's try to be more cordial, helpful, engaging and aware of our sur-roundings. Maybe, if we do, it might rub off on our children.

We can only hope!

Reflection: *Do you still open doors, or give up your seat, for an elderly person? If so, why? And if not, why not?*

Hey, Waddaya Gonna Do?

> Can any of you by worrying add a single moment to your lifespan? Do not worry about tomorrow; tomor-row will take care of itself. Sufficient

for a day is its own evil. Matthew
6:27, 34 (NAB)

Recently, I made contact through Facebook with an old friend, Tom
Occhipinti, from Youngstown, Ohio, who went to the same Italian
parish, Our Lady of Mount Carmel, as I did, until Diane and I
moved to Atlanta. I knew his parents, his older sister, Janice taught
my wife's faith formation classes, and Tommy credits me (a little)
for encouraging his career as a song writer. And, he is a very successful songwriter, now living in Nashville.

I checked out a very beautiful audio book entitled "Tools" that Tom
wrote and narrated. It's about his dad, John, who was a wonderful,
kind, Sicilian man, who always welcomed me and my family at
church functions.

Like many Sicilian immigrants, they were men of few words. Tom
recalls that whenever something bad would happen to a friend or
family member, like a death in the family, the loss of a job, divorce
or health issues, his dad would ponder for a long moment, look the
friend straight in the eyes and say, "Hey, whaddaya gonna do?"

That was it; it pretty much summed things up. I can remember when
I was a kid going to funerals of elderly family members, the men
would all line up to pay their respects. They would shake the be-
reaved persons hand, or hug and kiss them if they were family, pause
and say, "Hey, waddaya gonna do?"

Recently, I attended the calling hours for a young man that passed
away. He was from a wonderful family and we were friends with the
young man's parents. As we approached them in the line, I pondered in my mind the right thing to say to these grieving parents. As
I hugged and kissed the man's mother, I was speechless. When she
hugged me, she whispered in my ear, "Tony, waddaya gonna do?"
My tongue finally loosening, I replied, "I know. Waddaya gonna
do?"

Hundreds of books on compassion, anger, resentment, worry, and anxiety have been written by writers with a lot more education than John. But I'll tell you this, from all the books that I have read on these topics, nothing sums things up better than, "Hey, waddaya gonna do?"

Reflections: *Are you ever at a loss for what to say at a funeral? Are you fearful you might say the wrong thing? How uncomfortable are you in these situations?*

My Little Black Book

> And the prayer of the faithful will save the sick person, and the Lord will raise him up. If he has committed any sins, he will be forgiven. — James 5:15 (NAB)

Growing up in the 60's, I realized that no self-respecting bachelor would be caught dead without his little black book. The little black book was the place where he kept track of all the beautiful women he dated at the same time. The book would have a name, a number, (as in, she's a 10!), her city and her telephone number. Some would also note whether she was a good girl, or a bad girl!

I must admit, I never had a little black book, until now! And, my wife is aware of it and even approves!

On the nightstand, next to my bed, I keep my little black book. And like the bachelor's book in the 60's, it contains the names of many women. Only my little black book has the names of the women that I pray for, who are in prison, or have been released from prison. I have their name and a number. Only this time, the number is the number of years they are serving, and it has the name of her prison and her prison number. Society would say they were all bad girls, but I know better.

In my jail ministry, I meet many women inmates. Most come from dysfunctional families; many have little or no self-esteem, but most are decent women that simply made bad decisions. I always treat them with love and respect, the kind of love that most of them never got from a father, or grandfather.

Following their sentencing, and before they transfer to prison, some will hand me a slip of paper with their name, prison, number of years they will serve. And, they will ask me to pray for them. And I do pray for them.

I look at my list each week. Some have served their time and have been released. Others are still in prison. I can only hope that those who have served their time have gotten, or will get, some help to never return. For those women, I continue to pray each day.

My little black book contains other names as well. It has all the people I pray for, especially those who asked for my prayers.

Intercessory prayer is a powerful part of the communion of saints, and we can multiply the prayers going to God, through Jesus, by our commitment to praying for others. Why not start your prayer list today. You, too, can have your "little black book," and pray for those who have no one else to pray for them.

Reflections: *Do you believe in intercessory prayer? Do you keep a prayer list of people you pray for? Are you a member of a prayer circle? How does praying for others help you in your own faith journey?*

God Grants Mulligans

> If we acknowledge our sins, he is faithful and just and will forgive our sins and cleanse us from every wrongdoing. - 1 John 1:9 (NAB)

Every week, when I tee it up with my buddies, we have an unwritten rule that everyone gets a mulligan. A mulligan is basically a do-over, a second chance to redeem ourselves from a really bad shot.

God is that way with sin. We are all sinners and even with the best intentions, we continue to sin. But God gives us a mulligan, a second chance to redeem ourselves. In fact, our God is so awesome that he gives us unlimited do-overs. My buddies are not so generous!

When I speak at the jail, I tell the inmates that there is NO sin that God can't forgive. No sin is so great for our all-powerful, ever-loving God to forgive. We simply need to acknowledge and confess our sins and ask for his forgiveness with a humble, contrite heart as in Psalm 51:

> Have mercy on me, God, in accord with your merciful love; in your abundant compassion blot out my transgressions. Thoroughly wash away my guilt; and from my sin cleanse me. — Psalm 51:3-4 (NAB)

For many prisoners, this is the game changer; the one thing that brings them closer to Our Lord. Many believe that the crimes they committed, or the mistakes they made, are unforgivable. But God forgives every sin.

The only sins God can't forgive, I explain, are the one you don't ask Him to forgive. Think about it, if God is love, then forgiveness is assured.

Jesus took all our sins to the cross. He died for our sins, no matter how big, or how insignificant. He took all of them upon his shoulders.

It is also important for each of us to forgive those who hurt us. Forgiveness is the key, whether we ask for it, or give it.

> If you forgive others their transgressions, your heavenly Father will forgive you. But if you do not forgive others, neither will your Father forgive your transgressions. Matthew 6:14-15 (NAB)

Almost a year ago, I wrote about anger and resentment and the power of forgiving others. Included in that story was the forgiveness prayer. I can't begin to tell you how many people benefited from its powerful message. You can read it later in this book (Chapter 3).

The Lord offers us many things, among these are forgiveness, mercy, justice, and salvation. But it all begins with forgiveness.

Go ahead, ask God for a mulligan!

Reflection: Do you ever think that your sins are unforgivable? We all have core sins. Do you confess the same sins repeatedly? Does the fact that God forgives a humble sinner give you a feeling that, with God, you can do all things?

We All Need Validation

And a voice came from the heavens, saying, "This is my beloved Son, with whom I am well pleased." — Matthew 3:17 (NAB)

A year ago, a co-worker named Lyndse and I had a conversation about her father who had been diagnosed with a rare kidney disease. "His kidneys are shutting down," she confided, "and he might not make it to Christmas."

"We had one of the most important conversations of my life this weekend," she continued. "I finally, after all these years, received validation from my father. He told me that he was proud of me, and that I turned out well. I have been waiting all my adult life to hear him say that and now after that conversation, I realize that we might have only a short time together."

"At least you had the talk," I replied. "Imagine those people who lose a parent to sudden death who might never hear those words."

Validation from parents is a very important thing. Adult children long for it and even expect it. But often, they never receive the one gift from a father, or mother, that matters most - validation.

Why is it so difficult for parents to let their adult children know that they are proud of them, that they turned out well, that they have become good parents, great friends and people that matter?

As I looked at her sitting across from me in the office and crying, I spoke softly to her, "In reality, Lyndse, that validation might be the start of a dialogue that will continue. In your father's illness, you might be blessed with a better relationship, and share those things that you both love; art, music and your faith."

That conversation happened over a year ago. Lyndse's dad responded well to the experimental treatments. As the year progressed, most of the tumors were gone or shrinking, and just this past week the doctors reported that the cancer was gone!

Last Christmas passed, and another is fast approaching. Lyndse and her dad had many more conversations. Their relationship is growing slowly, and she feels good about the validation that she "turned out well." Knowing her as I do, I can echo those feelings, Lyndse turned out good, indeed!

That day, I learned two things: parents need to affirm to their children that that they turned out well. They need to do it now, and often. And secondly, we should use the time we have together to strengthen our relationships with the people that mean the most.

As Lyndse rose to leave my office that day, over a year ago, I sat back in my chair, closed my eyes and there in my thoughts was my deceased mother, smiling that special smile of validation as she gave me an affirming wink.

Reflections: *Have you given your adult children the validation they desperately desire?*

I Wish I was Your Daughter

> As a father has compassion on his children, so the LORD has compassion on the faithful. — Psalms 103:13 (NAB)

Years ago, I was asked to help coach a high school girls' soccer team. Up to this point, I only coached boys, and as a father with two sons and no daughters, coaching young women was a little scary for me.

I made some adjustments in my approach from years of coaching boys, and young men. I thought I was doing well, until the captains wanted to have a private meeting with me.

"Coach A.," one of the captains began, "You are a great soccer coach, but you've got to quit trying to be a father to us!"

A second captain, feeling less timid because now the subject was in the open added, "We already have a father meddling in our lives, we don't need two!"

Embarrassed, I agreed to comply with their wishes, and told them that I would do my best to just be a coach. The rest of the meeting was pleasant, and we talked about soccer only.

As the meeting broke up and the girls left, one of the captains, the one who had remained silent during the discussion, approached me.

"You don't have to change for me. I don't have a father. Your lending an ear, giving advice and just listening to me is something I never had as a young kid growing up. You are the closest thing I have to a father, so don't stop now."

I was reminded of this meeting during my jail ministry this past week. As our team waited in the classroom, four female inmates entered the room. I looked at them, and for some reason they all looked familiar.

I looked at the first and said, "You look very familiar to me. Do I know you?"

"Sure, Tony," she replied. "I have been here five times in the past eight years." The same thing was true for two of the other women; one had been in jail three times and another twice.

As we finished the prayer service and waited for the guard to arrive to take them back to the pod, the first woman said to me out of the blue, "I wish I was your daughter."

"Thank you," I replied slightly embarrassed. I am a father, but I only have sons, and a great daughter in-law!"

"Not so," she said correcting me. "Back in the pod, you have more daughters that you can imagine!"

"I do?" I said humbly. "Then, you can be my daughter, too!"

I had a warm feeling as we left the jail that night, and as we passed the laundry, I heard someone call out my name, "hi Tony!" It was another inmate I knew.

She told me that she had been sentenced to a year in prison but wanted to assure me that when she is released, she will be a changed person. Then she thanked me for my advice over the past several months, and for just listening.

No one cares how much you know,
until they know how much you
care. –Theodore Roosevelt [1]

I share these two stories, for two reasons.

First, one of the biggest failures in our society is the number of children, who grow up without a father, or father figure in their life. They long for a man who loves them unconditionally, cares for them more than life itself, a never wavering symbol of strength.

And secondly, YOU can be that person! As a teacher, coach, neighbor, uncle, or family friend, you can fill that void. And, many of you already are, and don't know it. Your example of listening, answering questions, giving advice, extending a hand, and being a non-judgmental, loving man, is having a bigger effect than you will ever know.

I pray for the day you, too, will hear those words, "I wish I was your daughter, or I wish I was your son!" For those of you who have, you will understand this feeling that I have that is impossible to explain, and why I pray every day for kids without fathers.

Reflections: *What can I do to be a father figure for someone in my life?*

An Irregular Guy

Father, God chose the foolish of the world to shame the wise, and God chose the weak of the world to shame the strong, and God chose the lowly and despised of the world, those who count for nothing, to reduce to nothing those who are

> something, so that no human being
> might boast before God. It is due to
> him that you are in Christ Jesus, who
> became for us wisdom from God, as
> well as righteousness, sanctification,
> and redemption, so that, as it is writ-
> ten, "Whoever boasts, should boast
> in the Lord." — 1Corinthians 1:27-
> 31 (NAB)

The seasons are changing, and for the first time this season, it was cold enough to wear a coat. As I scanned the coats in the hall closet, I spotted a nice-looking black coat that I never noticed before. I removed it from the hanger and saw that it still had the sales tags on it. It was new! My wife bought me a new coat, and I didn't even know it.

As I slipped the coat on, I noticed that it fit perfectly. But, to my dismay, as I went to zip it up, I noticed that the zipper was back-wards. It had been sewn in wrong. As I looked at the tag, my suspicions were correct. This wonderful coat was an irregular!

Irregular, a word from my youth, still stings when I hear it. I grew up in a blue-collar family. My mom did most of my clothes shopping in the bargain basement of the local men's store. She shopped in the "irregulars department."

As a naive kid, I never knew what an irregular meant. I thought it was a brand name! I can still remember the embarrassment. The kids at school were comparing their brand name clothes. "My shirt is an Izod," said one kid. "Mine is a Calvin Klein," said another. The dis-cussion went on until it was my turn.

"My shirt is an Irregular!" I proudly announced to a huge outburst of laughter. The laughter subsided as we made our way to class.

That night, I shared the story with my mom.

"What is an irregular?" I asked.

"Well, honey," she said as she paused to measure her words. "An irregular is a shirt, or pair of pants, with a slight flaw. Nothing big, or noticeable, but the prices are more affordable."

"You know son, the men Jesus picked for his apostles were all flawed. Each of the apostles were flawed in some way. And most of the saints didn't start out as saints. They were flawed, too, and they were able to overcome their flaws with God's grace."

She was doing her best to explain, but it wasn't working for me. I was still embarrassed to be the only kid in my class that was an irregular.

Now, as an adult, I can see the beauty in her wisdom. I realize that I am flawed. We are all flawed. For one thing, I am a sinner. And, only through God's grace and forgiveness, can I ever get to heaven.

I'm flawed in many other ways as well. I am balding and losing my hearing. I wear bifocal contacts, have bad knees, and a huge scar on my stomach from colon surgery. Come to think of it, I am a pretty irregular guy!

It is often said that God doesn't choose the qualified, he qualifies the chosen. I don't need to be perfect to serve Him. Just look at those apostles my mom mentioned. They were fishermen, tax collectors, men of no distinction. Yet, they went out and evangelized the entire world.

As I struggled to zip up my crazy zipper, I realized that being an irregular guy wasn't that bad. I'm going to wear my new jacket with humility and pride.

I know I'm flawed, but I'm happy to be an Irregular Guy!

Reflections: *Are you an irregular, too? Does salvation come from under-standing that we are all flawed, and thus in need of being saved?*

Not a Bead, But a "Glory Be!"

> 'For I know the plans I have for you,' declares the Lord, 'plans to prosper you and not to harm you, plans to give you hope and a future.' – Jer. 29:11 (NAB)

Several times a year, our parish does a living rosary. Each person represents a bead on the rosary, and they form a human chain around the entire church representing each decade. One by one, they approach the statue of the blessed mother and recite their Our Father or Hail Mary.

I attended several of these beautiful living rosaries over the years, but I never recall being asked to be a bead. I think I was an assistant bead once. That is a person who accompanies the bead but doesn't get to say anything. That's tough for me!

While I was humorously bemoaning the fact that I have been over-looked as bead material over the years, my friend, Deacon Roger overheard my whining.

He told me the story of a young boy who was also overlooked when the sisters at the school selected the kids to be beads at the school living rosary.

"Sister", he moaned. "I have never been a bead."

The wise and compassionate nun said, but you are a "Glory Be!"

A "Glory Be," the young man asked with a confused look on his face.

"Yes," sister replied. "Glory Be" is said on the chain between the beads, and we both know that the chain holds the entire rosary together! So, you have a very important role."

"That's it," I thought. Just like the little boy, I am a 'Glory be', and I can help hold the rosary together.

Now if I can only get over being picked last as a first grader playing "The Farmer in the Dell!" I guess I prefer being a 'glory be' to "the cheese!"

Reflections: Is there any background activity you are involved with, rather than being in the spotlight? Do you ever feel more gratitude when you are not in the limelight?

It Takes a Licking and Keeps on Ticking

Or what woman having ten coins and losing one would not light a lamp and sweep the house, searching carefully until she finds it? And when she does find it, she calls together her friends and neighbors and says to them, 'Rejoice with me because I have found the coin that I lost.' In just the same way, I tell you, there will be rejoicing among the

angels of God over one sinner who
repents. — Luke 15:8-10 (NAB)

It was dark as we made our way to the parking lot, following a recent board meeting in Cleveland. As I got to my car, I wanted to remove my sport coat to be comfortable for the long ride home.

Setting my iPad on the hood of my car, I removed my coat and opened the back door of my SUV. I hung my coat neatly on a hanger.

I returned and said my goodbyes to the group, entered the vehicle and made my way down Euclid Avenue for several blocks from 30th to 14th street near Playhouse Square. I drove the short distance down 14th to the entrance ramp for I-71. As I made my way up the ramp, I accelerated to get up to the speed limit.

As I accelerated, I noticed what looked like a leather case, about the size of an iPad, flying over my windshield over the roof of the car. As I glanced into my rear-view mirror, all I could see was this object, at least ten feet in the air, disappear into the darkness behind me.

"Oh, my God, it's my iPad," I realized! "I forgot it on the hood of my Chevy!"

I can't begin to tell you the hollow feeling I felt in my stomach, further complicated by trying to explain what had just happened to my wife, who I was talking to on the cell phone.

I hurriedly got off on the next exit, stopped my car and search the back seat, and the floor, even though I knew I wouldn't find it in the car. Making a U-Turn, I got back on I-71 and made my way to Jacobs Field, down Ontario, and cutting across to 14th street to re-track my route.

As I made my way back, I began to pray to St. Anthony, the patron saint of lost articles. I pray the St. Anthony prayer every day, but in my panic, I couldn't remember it. All I could remember was the simple little prayer that little children were taught.

Tony, Tony turn around. Help me find what can't be found.

As I approached the I-71 ramp, I turned on my bright lights and emergency flashers and slowly made my way up the ramp. It was very dark and there were weeds three feet high on both sides of the road. If it were in these weeds, it probably wouldn't be found for months. As I neared the top of the ramp, I saw a streetlight. It was shining like a spotlight at a rock concert on a small area of the berm, and there was my iPad!

I opened the door and scooped it off the blacktop and on to my passenger seat. Then, I quickly sped up to allow the other cars to enter the ramp.

As I made my way home, thanking God (and St. Anthony) for finding my iPad, with all of my personal data, prayers, notes for my book, e-mails and business information, I reached over to the passenger seat and pushed the button to turn on my device. I lit it up and it was working fine, except for the shattered screen.

I wish I could have prayed a more adult prayer, but it seems that St. Anthony likes this one just fine!

In case you are wondering, here is the St. Anthony prayer [2] I say daily but couldn't remember:

> O Holy St. Anthony, gentlest of
> Saints, your love for God
> and Charity for His creatures made
> you worthy, when on
> earth, to possess miraculous

powers. Miracles waited on
your word, which you were ever
ready to speak for those in
trouble or anxiety. Encouraged by
this thought, I implore
of you to obtain for me (request).

The answer to my prayer may require a miracle. Even so,
you are the saint of Miracles.
O gentle and loving St. Anthony,
whose heart was ever full
of human sympathy, whisper my
petition into the ears of the
Sweet Infant Jesus, who loved to be
folded in your arms, and
the gratitude of my heart will ever
be yours.

Reflections: *Did you recite the St. Anthony prayer when you lost an item? If you did so in your youth, do you still do it today? Do you have a problem with praying youthful prayers?*

How Do You Eat an Elephant?

O Lord, help me to remember that
nothing is going to happen today,
that you and I together, can't handle.
Amen. —Crystal Ayres [3]

Most of the incarcerated people I see have one thing in common; drug and alcohol abuse. No matter what crime they committed, the underlying problem is usually drugs, or alcohol, or both.

Whenever I speak to a group in jail, I like to ask a silly question.

"How do you eat an elephant?" I'll exclaim. After a few weird looks, a long moment of silence, and a few muffled laughs, I'll answer my own question.

"One bite at a time!" I offer.

After a few more seconds of silence, I'll ask one of the inmates, "What is your elephant?"

"Heroin," he'll reply with an embarrassing look on his face.

"And how are you going to eat this elephant?" I probe.

Then, as if a light bulb appears above his head, he replies, "One day at a time!"

"You've got it!" I'll excitedly confirm. "You win the battle against drugs one day at a time. For some, it's more difficult, it's one hour at a time, or one minute at a time. And, you can't do it alone. You need a higher power. God will help you."

You know the same holds true for all of us. We all face our own personal elephants! Sickness, disease, a bad marriage, financial difficulties, a job loss, all seem like problems that are too big for us to handle.

Truthfully, if we try to beat these challenges ourselves, they are too big for us to handle! But with God's help, we can break down these challenges into bite size forkfuls. The Holy Spirit will guide us if we call upon His help.

> No trial has come to you but what is
> human. God is faithful and will not
> let you be tried beyond your

strength; but with the trial he will
also provide a way out, so that you
may be able to bear it. — 1Corinthi-
ans 10:13 (NAB)

This verse doesn't mean we won't have problems, but it does say
that if you remain faithful, as God is faithful, he will provide you a
way out so that the problem will be bearable. Not alone, but with
God's help, this is possible.

Let me ask you, "What is your elephant?"

Reflections: *What is your elephant, and how are you going to deal with it
one day at a time? Drugs, alcohol and other addictions are best dealt with one
day at a time. Do you agree?*

The Giving Tree

Amen, I say to you, whatever you
did for one of these least brothers of
mine, you did for me. — Matthew
25:40 (NAB)

As we waited for Mass to begin, I noticed the Giving Tree had been
set up in the chapel. For the uninitiated, the Giving Tree is a Christmas tree decorated with paper ornaments with the name, age, and
sex of a needy person and something that they might like as a Christmas gift. Every year we take a few names and purchase gifts.

"Hey honey," I whispered. "We should get a few names from the
Giving Tree while there are still lots to choose from."

"Not today," my wife Diane responded. "I want to wait until they have been picked over. I like to buy for the people that no one picks; you know, the leftovers. I really like doing something special for the people no one picks."

As I settled back into my seat, I realized what she said. We are very judgmental people. We even judge what disadvantaged person gets our help. I have been guilty of this myself. I guess it is alright to pick a child, or a person of a particular sex, or in reading the notes, someone that we feel good helping. But there are always a few that no one selects.

I was so proud of Diane! I learn from her non-judgmental attitude. As a matter of fact, she prefers the unwanted, the leftovers, those who no one felt worthy.

It reminded me that one of my heroes, Mother Teresa, quickly became a saint for just that reason. She picked those that no one wanted, to help.

She would say, "If you judge people, you have no time to love them." [4]

This Christmas season let's try to be less judgmental and help those who become the leftovers on the Giving Tree.

Reflections: Have you ever been guilty of being judgmental when helping people? What do you think of Mother Teresa's observation that judging people gives us no time to love them? Do you participate in your Giving Tree?

Papa Charlie

> As you know, we treated each one of
> you as a father treats his children, ex-
> horting and encouraging you and
> insisting that you conduct your-
> selves as worthy of the God who
> calls you into the kingdom of his
> glory.— 1Thessalonians 2:11-12
> (NAB)

In 1997, in celebration of our twenty fifth wedding anniversary, Diane and I, and our two sons, Matthew and Mark, took a wonderful vacation to Italy.

Traveling to Italy had been a lifelong dream of mine, fueled by my mother's longing to return to the land of her roots. Mom planned to go to Italy many times, even getting her passport, but something always happened to cancel her plans. A death in the family, an illness, something always got in the way. She never made the trip, and I vowed that I would take it for her. I even brought her passport with us and had it stamped as we travelled throughout Europe.

One sunny afternoon in Rome, we decided to visit the beautiful museum, *Museo e Galleria Borghese*, on the grounds of the beautiful Villa Borghese. We loved the beautiful sculpture and were impressed that our son, Matt, recognized sculpture from masters like Canova and Bernini, particularly Bernini's masterpiece, *Abduction of Prosperpina by Plato*. There were paintings from Rubens and Raphael. It was magnificent! Matthew must have been listening that day at school.

114 A STORYTELLER'S GUIDE, VOL. 2

Alongside of the museum was a beautiful garden, one of many on the grounds and we decided to take a stroll while we waited for our ride back to the hotel.

As we walked, I spotted a cart with a vendor selling Lupini beans! For the uninitiated, Lupini beans are a snack food that you eat by tearing the skin of the soft shell and "popping" them into your mouth. They are served like French fries in a paper cone.

The vendor spotted me as I walked closer. *"Il mio amico, ti piace lupini fagioli?"* (My friend, do you like Lupini beans?)" He asked in Italian. *Sì, io li amo!"* (yes, I love them) I responded.

As I got closer, I was amazed at how much he looked like my father-in-law Papa Charlie, who we lost eight years earlier in 1989. He could have been his twin!

He carefully took the cone and filled it with our snack and reaching into his shirt pocket he produced an envelope. In the envelope was salt, which he sprinkled over the top.

Giving me a big grin, he handed me the cone and with a wink, he nodded at Diane saying, "enjoy them with your beautiful wife." (*Godetevi con la vostra bella moglie.)*

As I walked to the bench where Diane was now sitting to share the Lupini, I said, "That man could have been your dad!" As we both turned to get one more look at him, he and the cart were gone. Not a sign of them anywhere!

Almost simultaneously we realized that there were NO vendors in the park. We hadn't seen any before or after this encounter. I'm not certain if they are allowed to be there.

Was this a coincidence, an illusion, or just a man with a fast cart that could disappear quickly into the trees, we will never know. But we were both convinced that this WAS her dad. Or if not, then he was sent to us to tell us that Papa Charlie was at peace. Looking down from heaven, he was telling us how happy he was that for 25 years we shared our lives together.

On October 28, 2012, Papa Charlie would have been 100 years old. This past June, Diane and I celebrated our 40th anniversary. Papa Charlie would still be smiling.

Reflections: *Do you think that God gives us signs that deceased loved ones are at peace? Have you ever experienced what you thought was a sign from God? How did it make you feel?*

Save It for Easter

> Thus, you were adorned with gold
> and silver, and your dress was of
> fine linen, silk and embroidered
> cloth – Ezek. 16:13 (NAB)

Easter is the greatest holiday in the Christian church year. In the 1950's, the tradition of dressing up in your finest new clothes at Easter time was the norm. As a matter of fact, the tradition dates back many centuries.

According to the book "The Whole Earth Holiday," [5] the tradition began when early Christian converts were baptized at Easter and then given new white robes to wear for eight days. The Emperor Constantine ordered his subjects to dress in their finest clothes and parade in honor of Christ's resurrection.

That tradition of dressing up at Easter, attending the Easter parade, with men wearing suits, and women wearing hats and gloves are all gone now; things of the past. Now Easter Mass is no different than any other Sunday. You will see people in shorts, jeans, flip-flops, and tee shirts.

As a youngster, I remember on my birthday every year (in February, during or near Lent), I would always receive some article of clothing as a gift. Whether it was a sweater, a new shirt, pair of pants or a jacket, as I opened the gift, my mother would say, "Save it for Easter!"

Later that day, my aunt would see my birthday gift and would proclaim, "Anthony, that's a nice sweater. Save it for Easter!"

 All throughout the day, when family would see my birthday gift, I would hear the same response.

I never realized why it was so important to them that I wear something new at Easter Mass.

Now, as an adult I realize how important Easter was to my blue collar and very Catholic family. This was THE holiday of the year! And the banquet of food that we would enjoy after Mass was unbelievable. Everything was the best; the best clothes, best food, and best celebration, because we were celebrating the Resurrection of Our Lord, Jesus Christ. This was NO ordinary Sunday.

Think about it, if it wasn't for the Resurrection, our Christian faith would not exist.

> If there is no resurrection of the dead, then neither has Christ been raised. And if Christ has not been raised, then empty (too) is our

preaching, empty, too, your faith.
...And if Christ has not been
raised, your faith is in vain; you are
still in your sins. −1 Corinthians
15:13-14, 17 (NAB)

That is cause for celebration, the reason to put on your best clothes, to celebrate the Lord's Resurrection, the reason for our faith!

Next Sunday, let's leave the shorts, flip-flops, and blue jeans at home. Take the tags off that new sweater in your closet. Let's celebrate Easter as the most important day of the year.

My mom and my aunts are gone now, but to this day, my wife makes sure that on my birthday, I always receive something that I can "save for Easter."

He is Risen, Alleluia! Have a blessed Easter!

Reflections: *Is Easter just another Sunday to you and your family? What have you done to make Easter a special day? Have you explained to your kids the real meaning of Easter?*

The Seven Great Prayers

Pray without ceasing. − 1 Thess.
5:17 (NAB)

While returning home from the doctor, when you have just been diagnosed with colon cancer, many things go through your mind. Am I going to die? What will my wife do? Will our savings be wiped out? And, the list goes on.

Exhausted and totally defeated, I decided to do what I always do, bury myself in e-mail! The first e-mail I read got my attention quickly. Subject line: The *7 Great Prayers*.

As I read, the e-mail revealed the first of the seven prayers. The prayer was simply; **"I Love you God."** That's it. As I thought about it, I really haven't spent a lot of time telling God that I love him, but I realized that as a father, I needed to hear," I love you," so, I supposed God does, too.

It is like the conversation you have with your daughter, when she wants to borrow money for a new pair of shoes. The conversation goes something like this:

"I love you Daddy, you know, I really love you! (pause) Can I borrow $50 dollars?" The thing is, the strategy works every time!

So, I began to pray. "I love you God, I really want to serve you, but you've got to help me with this cancer. If I put the cancer in your hands, I could serve you better. Your will be done Lord. Know that I love you."

As I glanced down for the next prayer, the email said that I would receive it tomorrow and I would get one each day until I had received all seven.

The next day, I couldn't wait to see the prayer. It was simple as well.

The prayer was **"Thank you God for…."** I thought for a minute and began. Thank you, God, for an early diagnosis. Thank you, God, for a great doctor. Thank you, God, for a loving and supportive wife. The many thoughts of "thank you" continued for over 90 minutes! I simply thanked God for all the many blessings he gave me.

One by one, once a day I received the prayers. And they were an amazing help for me with tests, surgery, and recovery. I still pray them today, eight years later, cancer free.

Those prayers were sent to me by Paul McManus. How he got my name I'll never know, but they were a miracle each day. Paul later put these prayers into a book that he co-authored with his wife Tracey. [6] I shared only the first two with you because of time, but here are all seven prayers:

1. I Love You God

2. Thank You God for…

3. God, You are Inside Me

4. I Attract God's Blessings

5. God, I See You Everywhere

6. God Bless and I Love….

7. God, Let Me Do Your Good Works

I am sure they will help you, too. And, by the way, the book is terrific. I bought and gave away close to a hundred copies these past eight years.

If you face a health concern, relationship problems, a financial crisis, or just struggle with finding a purpose for your life, these simple 7 prayers might help find the answers you need.

Reflections: *Have you ever prayed one of these 7 prayers? If you have prayed a prayer of thanks to God, how did you feel when you finished? Are you tempted to try a few of these prayers?*

A Final Thought

And that's the end of the stories. I hope that one, or more, has been a blessing to you. If you enjoyed the stories in this book, please read my first two books, *A Storyteller's Guide to a Grace-Filled Life* and *A Storytellers Guide to Joyful Service*. I hope they will aid your search for growth in your faith and will assist you in growing closer to Our Lord.

All net proceeds from the sale this book, as well as the others, will go to the charities and ministries that I mention herein. I make no money from the sales of the books.

References

Chapter 1- God's Grace in Daily Life

[1] Holland, Kimberly. "Why a Lack of Sleep Can Make You Angry." Healthline.com. Dec 4, 2018. https://www.health-line.com/health-news/why-a-lack-of-sleep-can-make-you-angry#What-the-study-showed

[2] Paschal, Blaise. "Goodreads – Quotable Quotes." Good-reads.com. Accessed Jul 18, 2019. https://www.goodreads.com/quotes/801132-there-is-a-god-shaped-vacuum-in-the-heart-of-each

[3] Anonymous. "Goodreads-Quotable Quotes." Goodreads.com https://www.goodreads.com/quotes/tag/cherokee Accessed Jul 19, 2019.

[4] Kelly, Matthew. *Rediscover Catholicism. 2nd Ed.* Cincinnati: Beacon Publishing, 2002. p. 43

[5] *Ibid.* p. 43

[6] *Catechism of the Catholic Church, 2nd Ed.* Vatican City: Editrice Libreria Vaticana, 1997. Print. n. 2697.

[7] Teresa of Calcutta. "AZ Quotes – Mother Teresa." Azquotes.com. Accessed Jul 18, 2019. https://www.azquotes.com/quote/685911

[8] *Catechism of the Catholic Church, 2nd Ed.* Vatican City: Editrice Libreria Vaticana, 1997. Print. n. 2699.

[9] Dahl, Gordon. *Work, Play, and Play in a Leisure-Oriented Society.* Minneapolis: Augsburg-Fortress, 1972. Print. p. 23.

[10] Haugen, Marty. "All are Welcome in this Place." Songlyrics.com/MartyHaugen. Accessed Jul 18, 2019. http://www.songlyrics.com/marty-haugen/all-are-welcome-lyrics/

[11] Hunt, William Holman. *The Light of the World* painting. Circa 1900, housed at Saint Paul's Cathedral, London, England.

[12] Bryner, Jeanna, "Close Friends Less Common Today, Study Finds." Live Science. Nov 4, 2011. https://www.livescience.com/16879-close-friends-decrease-today.html

[13] *Ibid.*

[14] Francis. *Papal Address.* Vatican City: patheos.com. Dec 8, 2013. Accessed Jul 18, 2019. https://www.patheos.com/blogs/catholicnews/2013/12/pope-says-marys-whole-existence-is-yes-to-god/

[15] Kenyon, Sherrilyn. "Goodreads-Quotable Quotes." GoodReads.com. Accessed Jul 18, 2019. https://www.goodreads.com/quotes/171400-it-s-easy-to-look-at-people-and-make-quick-judgments

[16] Burkett, Jonathan Anthony. "Goodreads-Quotable Quotes." Goodreads.com. Accessed Jul 19, 2019. https://www.goodreads.com/author/show/1097709.Jonathan_Anthony_Burkett

[17] Coelho, Paulo. "Goodreads – Quotable Quotes." Good-
reads.com. Accessed Jul 18, 2019.
https://www.goodreads.com/quotes/22925-we-can-never-
judge-the-lives-of-others-because-each

[18] Warren, Rick "AZ Quotes." Azquotes.com. Accessed Jul 19,
2019. https://www.azquotes.com/quote/710859

[19] Wolpert, Stuart. "Here is What Real Commitment to Your Marriage Means." Los Angeles: UCLA Relationship Institute.
Feb 1, 2012. Accessed Jul 18, 2019.
http://newsroom.ucla.edu/releases/here-is-what-real-
commitment-to-228064

[20] Ibid.

[21] Thoreau, Henry David. "Goodreads – Quotable Quotes."
Goodreads.com. Accessed Jul 18, 2019.
https://www.goodreads.com/quotes/597758-what-you-get-by-
achieving-your-goals-is-not-as

[22] Saint Teresa of Calcutta. "Goodreads-Quotable Quotes." Good-
reads.com. Accessed Jul 19, 2019.
https://www.goodreads.com/quotes/252963-seeking-the-face-
of-god-in-everything-everyone-all-the

[23] Saint Teresa of Calcutta. Pinterest: quotes.lordsplan.com. Accessed Jul 19, 2019.
https://www.pinterest.com/pin/835769643318165525/

[24] Ibid.

[25] Augustine of Hippo. "Goodreads – Quotable Quotes." Goodreads.com. Accessed Jul 18, 2019. https://www.goodreads.com/quotes/126110-right-is-right-even-if-no-one-is-doing-it

[26] Francis of Assisi. (attributed quote). Focuscampus.org. Oct 4, 2011. Accessed Jul 18, 2019. https://focusoncampus.org/content/did-francis-really-say-preach-the-gospel-at-all-times-and-if-necessary-use-words

Chapter 2-Faith, Family, Friends

[1] Roosevelt, Theodore. "Goodreads – Quotable Quotes." Goodreads.com. Accessed Jul 18, 2019. https://www.goodreads.com/quotes/118880-no-one-cares-how-much-you-know-until-they-know

[2] "Unfailing Prayer to Saint Anthony." Christian-miracles.com. Accessed Jul 19, 2019. https://www.christian-miracles.com/saintanthonyprayer.htm

[3] Ayres, Crystal. "Prayer #4." connectusfund.org. Oct 8, 2018. Accessed Jul 18, 2019. https://connectusfund.org/25-powerful-short-prayers-for-hope-strength-and-faith

[4] Saint Teresa of Calcutta. "Goodreads-Quotable Quotes." Goodreads.com. Accessed Jul 19, 2019. https://www.goodreads.com/quotes/2887-if-you-judge-people-you-have-no-time-to-love

Acknowledgements

There are so many people to thank for their help in writing, editing and publishing The Storyteller's series.

That you to my editor Virginia Lieto, for her meticulous job in polishing my manuscripts and for proof-reading the final product. To Jeff Flaherty and Barbara Gaskell, for the rough edits.

To Chuck Everhart for the cover design, photography promotional graphics on all three of the books in The Storyteller's series.

To my wife Diane, for the encouragement and weekly spelling and grammar checks.

Thank you to the Catholic blogging community and the Catholic Writers Guild for their support.

And, a special thank you to my readers for the letters, emails, and social media comments that encourage me to continue my writing journey

.

God bless each of you with his abundant grace.

Other Books by Tony Agnesi

Web site: TonyAgnesi.com

A Storyteller's Guide to a Grace-Filled Life, Tony Agnesi, Wadsworth: Virtu Press, 2017.

A Storyteller's Guide to Joyful Service: Turning Your Misery into Ministry, Tony Agnesi, Wadsworth: Virtu Press, 2018.

Made in the USA
San Bernardino, CA
10 January 2020